Unwritten Letters Project

Dear Mom Dear You Dear Me *Dear Universe* Dear Best Friend Dear Brother De
cle Ben Dear World Dear Alex Dear Someone I Used to Know Dear Manager Dear Cat I
Future Dear Mom Dear You Dear Me Dear Universe Dear Best Friend Dear Brother Dea
cle Ben Dear World **DEAR ALEX** Dear Someone I Used to Know Dear Manager Dear Ca
Future Dear Mom Dear You Dear Me Dear Universe Dear Best Friend Dear Brother Dea
cle Ben Dear World Dear Alex Dear Someone I Used to Know Dear Manager Dear Cat I

Future Dear Mom Dear You Dear Me Dear Universe **Dear Best Friend** Dear Brother
Uncle Ben Dear World Dear Alex Dear Someone I Used to Know Dear Manager Dear C;
Future Dear Mom Dear You Dear Me Dear Universe Dear Best Friend Dear Brother Dea
cle Ben Dear World Dear Alex **DEAR SOMEONE I USED TO KN**
Dear Manager Dear Cat Dear Future Dear Mom Dear You Dear Me Dear Universe Dear
Friend Dear Brother Dear Uncle Ben Dear World Dear Alex Dear Someone I Used to Kr

Dear Manager **DEAR CAT** Dear Future Dear Mom Dear You Dear Me Dear Universe
Best Friend Dear Brother Dear Uncle Ben Dear World Dear Alex Dear Someone I Used
Know Dear Manager Dear Cat Dear Future Dear Mom Dear You Dear Me Dear Universe
Best Friend Dear Brother Dear Uncle Ben Dear World Dear Alex Dear Someone I Used
Know Dear Manager Dear Cat *Dear Future* Dear Mom Dear You Dear Me Dear
verse Dear Best Friend Dear Brother Dear Uncle Ben Dear World Dear Alex Dear Some
Used to Know Dear Manager Dear Cat Dear Future Dear Mom Dear You Dear Me Dear
verse Dear Best Friend Dear Brother Dear Uncle Ben Dear World Dear Alex Dear Some
Used to Know *Dear Manager* Dear Cat Dear Future Dear Mom Dear You Dear
Dear Universe Dear Best Friend Dear Brother Dear Uncle Ben Dear World Dear Alex De
Someone I Used to Know Dear Manager Dear Cat Dear Future Dear Mom Dear You Dea
Dear Universe Dear Best Friend Dear Brother **DEAR UNCLE BEN** Dear World Dear
Dear Someone I Used to Know Dear Manager Dear Cat Dear Future Dear Mom Dear Yc
Me Dear Universe Dear Best Friend Dear Brother Dear Uncle Ben Dear World Dear Ale
Someone I Used to Know Dear Manager Dear Cat Dear Future Dear Mom Dear You Dea

Dear Universe Dear Best Friend *Dear Brother* Dear Uncle Ben Dear World Dear Alex
Someone I Used to Know Dear Manager Dear Cat Dear Future Dear Mom Dear You Dea
Dear Universe Dear Best Friend Dear Brother Dear Uncle Ben Dear World Dear Alex De
Someone I Used to Know Dear Manager Dear Cat Dear Future Dear Mom Dear You Dea
Dear Universe Dear Best Friend Dear Brother Dear Uncle Ben Dear World Dear Alex De
Someone I Used to Know Dear Manager Dear Cat Dear Future Dear Mom Dear You Dea
Dear Universe Dear Best Friend Dear Brother Dear Uncle Ben *Dear World* Dea
Dear Someone I Used to Know Dear Manager Dear Cat Dear Future Dear Mom Dear Yc
Me Dear Universe Dear Best Friend Dear Brother Dear Uncle Ben Dear World Dear Ale
Someone I Used to Know Dear Manager Dear Cat Dear Future Dear Mom Dear You Dea
Dear Universe *Dear Best Friend* Dear Brother Dear Uncle Ben Dear World D
Alex Dear Someone I Used to Know Dear Manager Dear Cat Dear Future *Dear Mon*
You Dear Me Dear Universe Dear Best Friend Dear Brother Dear Uncle Ben Dear Worlc
Alex Dear Someone I Used to Know Dear Manager Dear Cat Dear Future Dear Mom De
Dear Me *Dear Universe* Dear Best Friend Dear Brother Dear Uncle Ben Dear Worl

An *Unwritten Letters Project* **Book compiled by** ALEX BOLES

LeClere BOOKS LLC

UNWRITTEN LETTERS PROJECT. Copyright © by Alex Boles. Cover art by Brandi Kapfer. All rights reserved. Printed in the United States of America. No part of this book may be used or reproduced in any manner whatsoever without written permission except in the case of brief quotations embodied in critical reviews and articles. For information, contact LeClere Books LLC, PO Box 27890, St. Louis, MO 63146

This book is dedicated to my Family Communication class. Without you I would not have the inspiration to create this project.

~ Alex

TESTIMONIAL:

The Unwritten Letters Project is a collection of concentrated raw feelings. This is what's really going on under the surface, under our years of social conditioning. And collectively, I think, it speaks a truth about all of us: We're alive, darn it, and we have something to say!

I've written more than fifteen letters since I discovered the project, some less anonymous than others. The blog is an extension of my journal; these are the things I want to shout at the world. This project has been with me through relationships, sticky acquaintances, and tests of faith. It has witnessed my musings about the world around me.

The reason I keep coming back is this: I hope that, through my half-baked notions, just maybe someone will find a glint of wisdom that they can benefit from. There's a small chance that I could infect someone with a new idea. Sure, I want my viewpoint to be heard, but above all I hope that I can humbly offer insight. And I draw from all the other writers' insights as well.

So cheers to all the honest feelings! Cheers to the pain, infatuation, disgust, hope, love, and hatred expressed in these letters. Cheers to those who choose to read them and empathize with their fellow human beings. Cheers to us for exposing our jugulars and taking the time to create proof of our collective consciousness.

Sincerely Everyone's,

Laura Beth

INTRODUCTION:

Dear Readers,
In the spring of my junior year in college I worked through the idea of creating a website where people could submit letters to anyone and everyone they could possibly think of. I wanted people to get the same kind of satisfaction out of it that I was experiencing. Writing letters to people was always a mode of release for me growing up and I wondered if I was alone in this method of expressing my emotions. Turns out, I wasn't.

I know that Unsent Letters makes more sense, but the premise behind the name is that the letters are unwritten initially and when you're inspired, you write it, submit it and the world absorbs your emotions. The project started with a few notes and ideas scribbled on a piece of notebook paper in my Family Communication class, but turned into a world-wide phenomenon that is gaining more followers each day.

I've always clutched my desire to be involved in the literary world and I have now found an outlet not only for myself, but people around the world. It's been less than one year since the website started up and I receive a constant flow of letters, comments and support from family, friends and strangers. I cannot thank everyone enough for your continued support. Without the followers of the project, my family and my University, I would not be where I am today.

I want the Unwritten Letters Project to be a voice of the people. I want it to be a medium for people to express any emotion without the fear of being censored or judged. I do not allow negative comments on the website creating a comforting community for the writers and readers.

Even now I find myself writing letters whenever I feel inspired. Although I plan to start working on numerous novel ideas and screenplays for the future, I plan to keep the Unwritten Letters Project up and running as long as there is interest and a letter in my inbox.

Thank you for everything.

Love,
Alex Boles

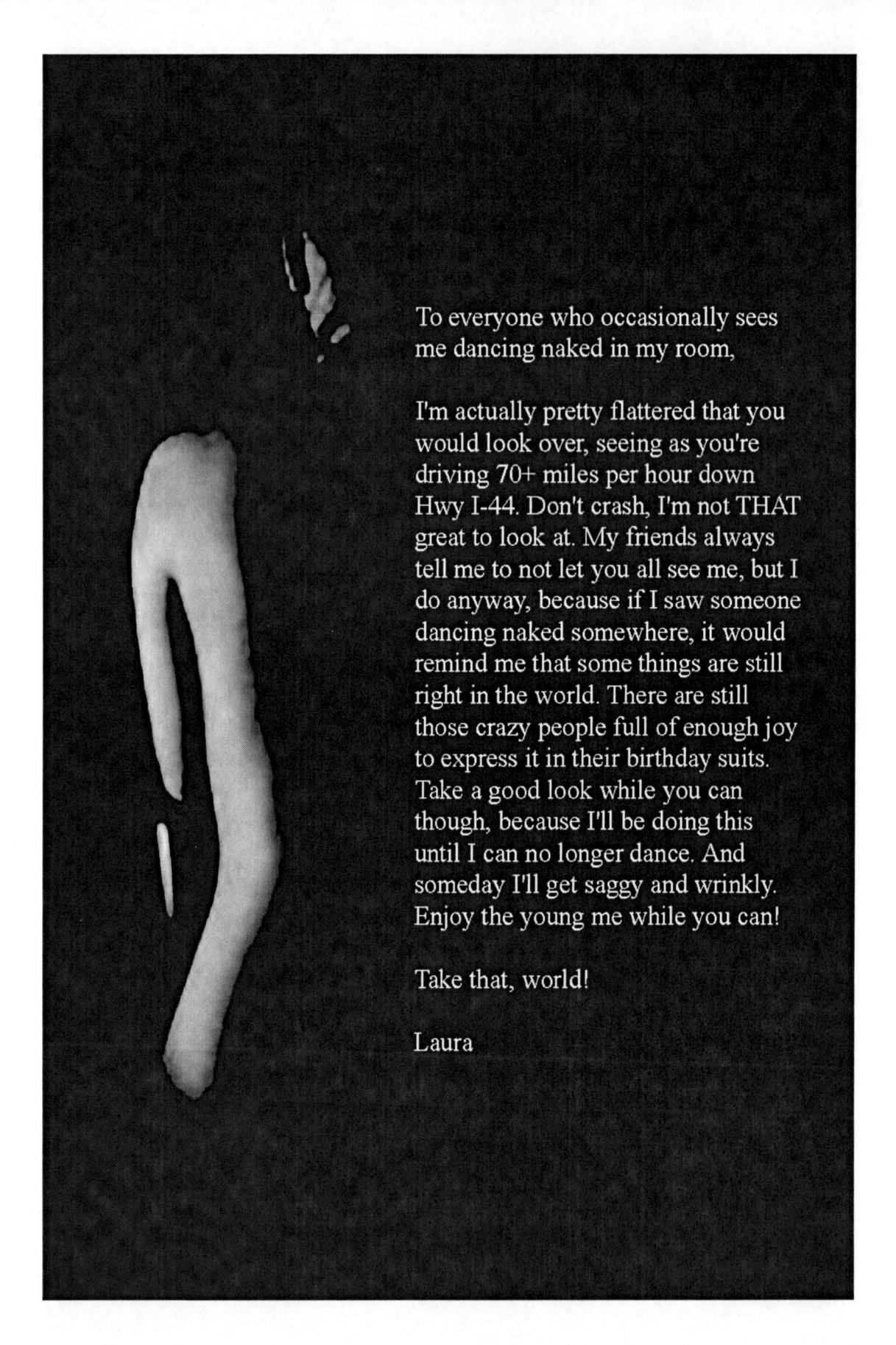

To everyone who occasionally sees me dancing naked in my room,

I'm actually pretty flattered that you would look over, seeing as you're driving 70+ miles per hour down Hwy I-44. Don't crash, I'm not THAT great to look at. My friends always tell me to not let you all see me, but I do anyway, because if I saw someone dancing naked somewhere, it would remind me that some things are still right in the world. There are still those crazy people full of enough joy to express it in their birthday suits. Take a good look while you can though, because I'll be doing this until I can no longer dance. And someday I'll get saggy and wrinkly. Enjoy the young me while you can!

Take that, world!

Laura

Dear anyone that has tried to help me,

I'm sorry for lying, stealing, and screwing up bad. Who would have ever known a drug could affect someone's life forever? If I were to know what I know now about heroin, there is no chance I would have ever done it, and what bothers me the most is I only did it to be with "him." "He" is worthless. I should have known a 23 year-old high school dropout living at home with his grandparents with no education nor job would not benefit me any. I'm sorry for stealing from my friends but mostly my parents. Twelve thousand dollars is a lot of money, and I regret every cent of it because I have nothing to show for it. I'm sorry for being such a messed up teenager, but mostly what no one knows is that I'm sorry I didn't die out of all the times I overdosed.
-Worthless Addicted Liar

Dear Life,
It's sad how things change.
Love, me

Dear people I see every day at my university,

I'd really like to meet you. I see you now and then, and some of you know my name by now, but I've never gotten to know any of you in the year that I've been here. I know it's really my own fault for being so shy, but it would mean the world to me if you would start a conversation with me sometime. I know I'm overweight, awkward, and just all around weird, but I can carry on a conversation, if you'll help me by starting one. Having someone to hang out with sometime would be a great alternative to spending the evenings sitting alone in my apartment.
Conure

Dear World,

I love you! I love your imperfections! I love how we humans rejoice when we feel the music or are inspired by something. I love the music we sing, the books we write, the structures we build. I love how tiny we are and how we think we know so much. I love that Mother Nature lovingly, but sternly puts us back in our place when we think we've conquered her. I love how we dream. I love that we share a common soul, that we have the capacity to love each other. I love that we never learn our lessons, but are endearing enough anyway that the soul of the Earth doesn't wipe us off the face of the planet. I love how the earth nourishes us, how we nourish each other. I love that we are allowed to spend roughly a little under a century learning everything we can about this wonderful place. I love you, I love you, I love you! I love that we dance and sing and offer it all up to something we don't even understand, something that is much greater than any names we give it and the restrictions we try to squeeze it into. I love our cultures, our differences, our similarities, our fears, our silly behaviors, and the fact that we really are animals, but that we really do think and wonder. I'm in love with everything about you, World. All the people, rocks, water, spiders, kangaroos, clouds, babies, temples trees, and little chances you provide us every day to be inspired.

Sincerely,
Your daughter, sister and friend

From one lost soul to another,

I think we need to re-think what gets taught at school these days, because in no way does it prepare you for reality.
In no way, are we taught that it's going to be this hard. That there are going to be so many times that we're going to want to give up, but that we need to keep holding on, because somewhere out there, there's someone waiting to help us, and we just need to hang on until they find us.
In no way are we taught that there are unimaginable terrors that we don't realize could ever happen to us until they happen. They don't tell you that your grandfather and your best friend might die within three days of each other when you're thirteen years old.
And when you realize it that young, from pure experience, where do you go from there? How do you possibly maintain the strength to keep moving forward and go to school to learn nothing of value. I don't know.
They don't tell you that achieving your dreams is so much more complicated than it would seem. That sometimes there will be absolutely no one who believes in you. And they don't teach you how to deal with it. They tell you to follow your dreams and have a smart plan, and they teach you how to make this plan, but how do you move forward and put this plan in action when everybody around you is against it?
Since we're not taught, how do we deal? I'm so lost, and I don't know what to do. And, maybe I just need some sort of sign, just a little one from God, to let me know how.
Am I the only who realizes this? How come we're not taught useful things like this in school? I just don't understand how we aren't, to be honest. I mean, you think someone who have realized by now, that maybe today's youth is becoming so corrupt because we're just lost with no direction. In order for use to be successful or strong we just need some direction, some guidance, something, or someone.

Dear Matt,

You are a stranger who walked into my life by chance. I would have never joined that website had I not been feeling unappreciated in my relationship. And you came along and gave me the courage to end something that meant so much to me...but yet, wasn't right for me and wasn't making me happy. As a complete stranger, even you saw it. I am forever grateful for that.

The first night you called me, even though I didn't say a word because I was so nervous, was pretty amazing. I fell for you and hard. Your voice alone is just so calming, and I can imagine it still when you IM me.

The first time I met you, I sat at the train station waiting and literally shaking from nerves. I was so scared that I was doing something completely stupid and wrong...but as soon as I saw you and you held me until I calmed down, I knew that day would be perfect. And it was. I didn't want you to leave.

So, I came to see you. Again, I was so nervous driving those three hours to stay the night with a guy I had met once. Was I crazy? Probably. Others would say most definitely. But, once again, everything was great. It felt like I had known you for years. And I still do.

Do I have feelings? Maybe. I'm not really sure. I know you want me to come and see you again, and I really don't have the money. But I'm also afraid that I'll get too attached again, and I know you need someone closer geographically for emotional support. I know I just can't provide that...But you are truly a magnificent person, and I greatly appreciate you, maybe more than you'll ever know.

Sincerely,
The "crazy" girl you spent the day at the arch with

lol :)

12

Dear Boy,

Thank you for asking me to dance at prom so many years ago. I will forever remember "Iris" as our song, even though I haven't had a decent conversation with you in several years.

On prom night, I was fully prepared to pretend like I didn't care that I didn't have anyone to dance with because I didn't have a date and had come with just a few girlfriends. So when you came up and asked ME, not the two other girls I was standing with, to dance, I was really touched. You had crossed the room to get to me, and that meant a lot.

My relationships with guys throughout the years have been, well, non-existent for the most part. So, when I've watched one too many chick flicks and just wish I had a boyfriend, the thought of you asking me to dance on prom night makes me feel a little better and gives me hope that someday maybe I'll find someone who's willing to cross the room for me again.

Sometimes I still imagine that perhaps, maybe, it could be you, and we would end up together.

Love,
Girl

∎ ▪

Dear Jesse Lacey,
Your music saved me. Thank you so much!

Love,
Karina

∎ ▪

Dear little girl in the back seat of the van in the drive thru who told me I was pretty,

Thank you. You made my day. The memory has made my day many times over the past three and a half years. I've never really thought of myself as pretty or that anyone else would think of me as pretty, so you thinking I was and saying so was really unexpected and heartwarming. I'm sorry I didn't respond more appropriately than telling you that you were pretty too and asking what your name was. I feel like that really trampled the innocence and genuineness of your comment. I'm also sorry that I didn't remember your name – you'd think I'd remember something like that. You really are pretty though, especially on the inside. I'll never forget you.

And tell your mom I said thanks, too, for rolling down your window.

K.S.

Dear Admissions Tutor,

I realize you have a tough job and I understand that sometimes you have to turn people down. But this time I think you made a big mistake.

I might not have met your entry requirements, and I might not have the most amazing portfolio or the best interview technique. But I do have passion and determination to succeed.

Proof of my determination is the improvement in my exam results from last year to this. I went from having 2 C's and a D to having 2 B's and a C. This improvement meant I had to take a two year English course in just one year. If that isn't determination and proof of hard work, I don't know what is.

There is nothing I wanted more than to come and study Journalism at your university. The whole time I've been thinking about university, Bournemouth is the only one I've ever cared about.

To be perfectly honest, I could have dealt with your rejection if you hadn't kept me holding on, building my hopes for an extra 24 hours, only to tear them down in a matter of seconds over the phone.

You think I can't do this. You think I'm not going to succeed. Well, I'll show you. You're wrong. Someday you'll see my name as editor of an international publication, and then you'll kick yourself. You'll realize that you should never have turned me down. Just because you say I can't do this does not mean that that it is true. I am not going to let that hold me back. I will be greater than you can imagine.

I hope that someday you will realize your mistake in turning me down.
Yours sincerely,
Natalie C

··

Dear Journey,

THANK YOU for being the best band EVER. :D You're the greatest.

- #1 Fan :)

··

Dude,
Stop showing up late for class. It's embarrassing. Don't you have any sense of pride? Self-respect? Do you know how embarrassing you are? It's insulting to the professor, and it's really annoying for everyone to deal with everyday. Ughhh. It's so pathetic. Please stop. I hate being reminded of your existence. Stop. And turn off your cell phone.
-J

Dear Commenter,

I am such a wimp. I started composing a comment to follow up your comment on Her blog post about how tough it is to show up at a gym when you're overweight...but I chickened out. Do you care if I share it with you anyway? First off, you're awesome for making time to get to the gym. I can never seem to prioritize well enough to get around to it. I am so out-of-shape it's not even funny. I need to get serious about my health.

On to my purpose here. It made me a little sad, a little frustrated, a little ticked off when I read your comment which repeatedly referred to thin people who exercise as 'stupid skinny people.'

So, here it goes: We're not all stupid. Even us skinny people have issues. I am probably more out of shape than most of the people you see in a day, and I have struggled my entire life with being UNDER weight. (I know, poor me, being too skinny. I get that all the time. It's why I usually don't say anything.) I am a stick of a person, and I can't help but wonder how nice it would be to find a top that fits - even sort of - in the WOMEN'S section. I am darn near close to 40 years old, and I have never been able to shop in the Women's clothing section. Does that make me less of a woman? Size-wise, I guess you could say YES. I don't like shopping in the junior's section because I look like one of those ladies who is still living in the past and can't accept that she's an adult now and needs to dress like one. I hate that my oldest daughter wears a larger size than me (she's 14 years old and wears a 5... a FIVE!) and feels fat because she wears bigger clothes than her mom. Do you think I enjoy that? Because I don't. I HATE it, and I don't use the word HATE lightly. I also HATE that I have to shop for bras in the little girl's section. Can you imagine how embarrassing that is? I can't wear shorts or capri pants because I can't stand all of the comments I get on my "chicken legs". Any time I bring up the fact that I need to start exercising to my friends, I get a few eye rolls along with comments about how I just need to eat more. How no one wants to exercise with me because I'm skinny. I can't even find anyone who wants to walk (for exercise) with me because they're sure I'll be too fast. I could go on and on, but it hurts, so I won't.

You hate being overweight? Being stick skinny isn't exactly a walk in the park, either. We all have our issues. Let's just treat each other as equals and look beyond size. Please?

If you don't call me stupid, I won't call you ignorant.

Sincerely,
Chicken Legs

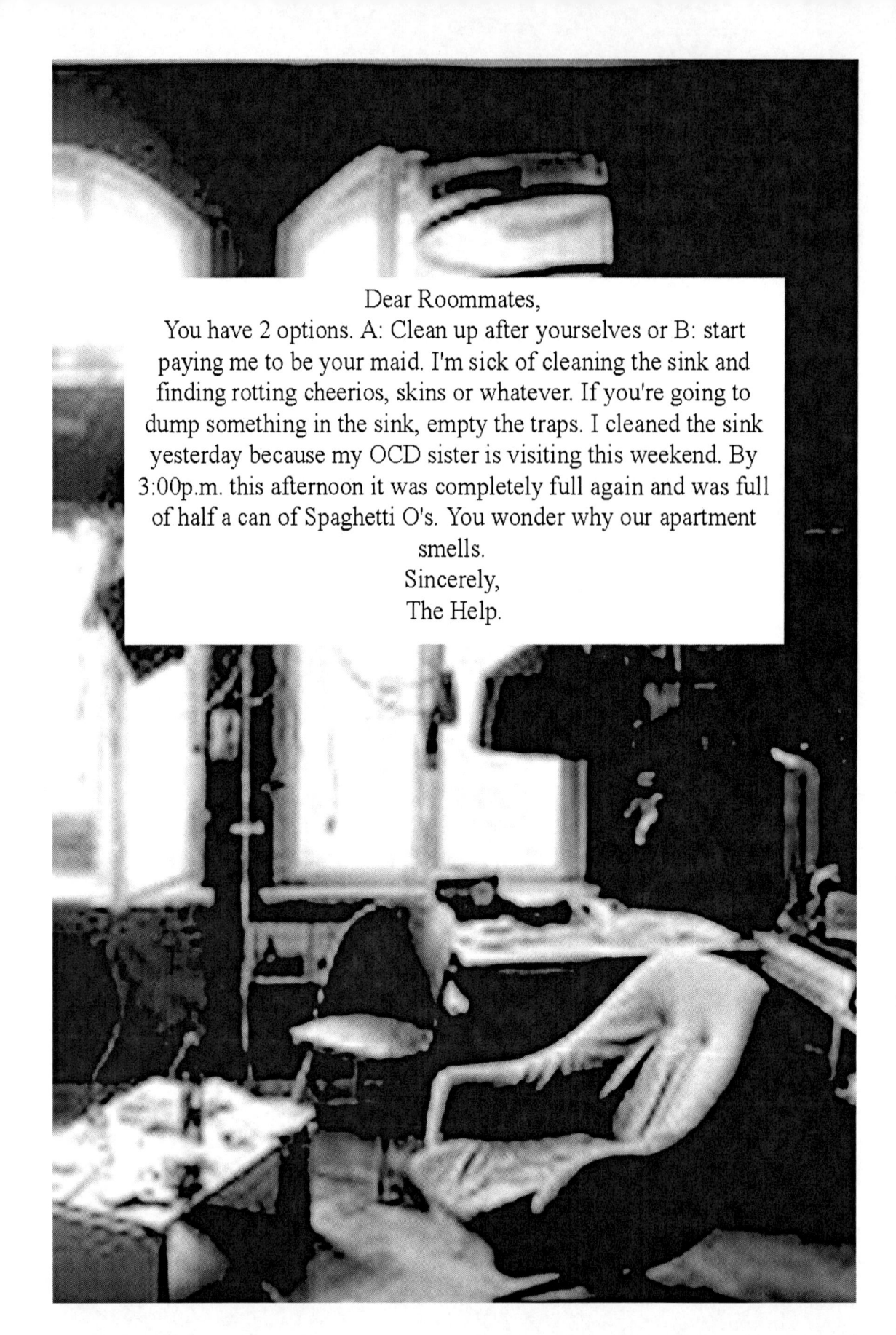

Dear Roommates,
You have 2 options. A: Clean up after yourselves or B: start paying me to be your maid. I'm sick of cleaning the sink and finding rotting cheerios, skins or whatever. If you're going to dump something in the sink, empty the traps. I cleaned the sink yesterday because my OCD sister is visiting this weekend. By 3:00p.m. this afternoon it was completely full again and was full of half a can of Spaghetti O's. You wonder why our apartment smells.
Sincerely,
The Help.

Dear friend,

It's just hitting you now that this is it. You're almost gone, and it's the end of the road. But what you don't understand is how much grieving I did already. It seems like you're just now catching up. Here's what I could never say to you in person: you left **me**. I'm not saying that in an accusatory manner, it's just how it happened: you're the one who left. And when I came back I had this new roommate who wasn't you, possibly the furthest thing from you, and that sucked. I really, really missed you and I still do. Talking to you on the phone and texting was ok but having you around all of the time to exchange stupid stories and watch our shows and stay up ridiculously late talking, helping each other overanalyze texts and give each other the most custom-made advice in the world and be able to go *anywhere* together and have a good time and making it to Shitty's at the end of the night (or not)…all that was so much better.
And honestly, I also didn't love talking to you on the phone because you made me feel like your new life was so grown-up and exciting and mine is just the same old shit, not even worth discussing. And when you came to visit, it was the same. I never realized how boring my life was to you until I noticed that you don't even ask anymore. I guess at some point I stopped trying. I know that was my fault. But you said it's the end of an era, and you're right. The era ended when you left, and I wish you would stop trying to blame me for what has happened to us.

Sincerely,

Me

Dear Alex,

You were the best friend I have ever had. I still just sit back and think about all the amazing times we spent together. We always had so much fun even if we weren't doing anything. You were hilarious and very loving. But then we changed. We got older and slowly started to discover ourselves. We started hanging out with people that were closer to our newly found personalities, leaving little space for one another. I know that's what happens to all childhood friendships, but I hate that it happened to mine. I hate that when I finally discovered what I had let happen, you were gone. I was lost, because you were lost. I had no way of getting a hold of you, and I had no idea where you were.

And I finally found you. But it feels as if it's too late. I'm still too different to keep my childhood friend. It's sad -- the world, the way we change. We lose who we are so simply. Like for boyfriends. Well at least that's what it has always been for me. Boys, stupid boys. And I still do it.

I'm sorry I wasn't a better friend. I'm sorry that I didn't hesitate to replace you with a boy I had a school-girl crush on. If I could go back, I would change it. I promise.

I love you forever and always,
Amy

Dear You,

I'm not sure if I ever got to tell you how much I loved you and how much fun I always had with you. I always looked forward to going to Maine every summer because I got to see you! I am so sorry that we didn't go to Maine the summer before you died. I often wonder if maybe you wouldn't have taken your life if we would have gone to Maine that summer. I really regret not going. I wish I could have said goodbye and that I love you. I wish that you were still here and that we could still spend part of our summers together. I love you!

Love,
Me

Dear Squid,
I really do love you. But a couple days ago I got closure and an apology that I was waiting for desperately. I can finally see the finality of our relationship, which can be nothing more than a deeply connected, weirdly intimate, amazing friendship. Even though you are about to take a huge step and move what seems like a million miles away, I can almost feel your fun, spunky presence bouncing beside me as I write this letter; although I look over and all that remains is air. I will not be able to laugh with you, cry on your shoulder, slap your arms playfully when you're being inappropriate, or read smutty gay comics with you on park benches. There is so much life that I'm going to miss out on, now that you are persuing your life with the man you love, because you are the essence of life. You live and breathe it; you are fun, spontaneous, and a little bit reckless and laugh like every laugh will be your laugh. While you are not super human and do have those down days, even then you refuse to let it hold onto you, unlike me. You know how passionate I am, and even sometimes that passion is my undoing, because I live, love and emote passionately, which can lead to great moments of sadness and despair. But, you are patient with me, you allow me to release the dams and drown you with my pent up emotions and frustrations and, like a great friend, you drink it in and throw me a life raft. I very much use the other tactic. Recently (as of when you started obsessing over your new beau) I have begun to take a different approach (as you well know) I am short, blunt and to the point and am not afraid to tell you to cut the crap. While this has caused you to lash out in certain instances, I believe that it has helped, I KNOW it has helped, because being around a crowd that is unwilling to tell you the truth about your actions is worse than one person telling you that they think you're being an asshole. Even in all the moments when I lose my grip and can't hold it together, you bring out the duct tape and make sure I'm structurally sound. Even when I believed I was broken, you didn't. You reminded me what it was like to feel whole. You reminded me how to just be and not worry about how to live, but to just live. I hope that one day, when we're old, crazy and grey-that we'll get a chance to see our grandkids laughing and playing and being just as good friends as we were, because the world needs more friends like you and I, so we might as well start a movement of our own.
Here's to wheelchair races and dying on the same day,
The Eagle.

Heather,

Do you remember me? Samantha. From first grade, when we were still friends. I'm sure you remember, Heather.

But do you also remember the trifle that ended our short friendship after almost exactly two years? That pink jacket, or was it a sweatshirt. Me, I don't remember exactly what happened; but then, I never found out the real truth. Was it Laura's sweater and she claimed you had ruined it by drawing on it with a pen, yet refused to pay for it – or was it the other way around? Fact is, after the summer holidays, I met Laura first and completely unaware of what had happened. And that, as I was to find out very soon, was the end of our friendship.

Yet what is broken can often be repaired; what is destroyed can often be built again. That sweatshirt is not the only thing standing between us; the other obstacle is the time that has passed, time of "non-friendship" – but I believe it's not too late yet. Let's be friends again. Friends like girls among girls. Not more – but not less, either.

You probably don't know that I vowed never to use those party bottles filled with colorful pieces of paper again before our friendship has been restored. You probably don't know how hard I prayed the following year before we moved away, perfectly aware of the fact that I was running out of time, yet feeling paralyzed as soon as I saw you, like that one time you passed by with Felicity – the only person who was your friend and my friend – as I was trying to climb a tree. You probably don't know that Laura once said she wouldn't mind if you died – that was shortly after the incident with the sweatshirt, but later felt sorry. You probably don't know that I continued praying long after we had seen each other for the last time – probably on the school yard or during lunch, when I sometimes tried to look you in the eyes, but it never worked – and I am still continuing to do so.

Now you know.

Heather, I'm serious: Can we please be friends again? Let's not let the past stand like a wall between us. Please! Think about it, Heather. And, please, answer me in any case. I'll be waiting for your reply.

Sammy

Dear Best Friend,

I wish we could be the way we were in sixth grade. You are beautiful, sweet, caring, fun, and smart. I miss everything about you. How am I supposed to tell you how I feel, now that you are leaving for Virginia? I am in love with you and would marry you right now, given the chance. I miss playing 20 questions with you. I know you don't feel the same way about me, and it hurts. I fall asleep thinking about you just so I can dream about you. Then when I finally have that dream, I try to not wake up. You have always been there for me, and I want to thank you for that. I have always been there for you, and I know you appreciate it. But now you are moving on, starting a new chapter of your life and leaving me behind. I am going to miss you so much.

Remember when we talked about the future and how we were going to have our kids call us "Aunt" and "Uncle", even though we aren't related? I want my kids to call you "Mom". You would be the best mother in the world. You are always talking about God and how great He is. Yes, He really is amazing. I just wish that He had planned for us to be together.

I am really going to miss you. Please be safe in Virginia. Don't forget about me. I will always answer your call, text, or email. I will always love you.

Dear you,

I'm sorry I can't come to the party next week. In fact, I don't think we should hang out again. It's not that I don't like you or want to be friends, but it's the simple fact that you keep pushing me into social situations. When are you going to be willing to learn that I'm not a social person? I've told you time and time again, but I don't think we can be friends any more.

You've been the best friend I could have ever had, but I can't let you keep pushing me into being around people. When I need people, I'll be around them. But not now and not when I don't want to be around them.

So please stop inviting me to things and surprising me with parties.

Love,
Me

Dear W.,

I'm sorry for having been such a disappointing friend to you. I haven't given you the attention and appreciation you've wanted from me, so I'm going to end the mutual frustration with each other by gradually letting our friendship fade. I've recently begun cutting ties little by little, though you probably realize that. I just don't have the energy to maintain what we had, and, at this point, I'm not sure we'll be able to manage much more than a certain level of civility.

I know I've made you angry for many reasons. I'll grant that I agree with you on some of these. For others, I still stand my ground. I won't let it bother me that you think I'm the most selfish person you know. I know who I am, and I know I have a heart. Right now I'm so spent that I can't expend the effort to prove you wrong.

I do hope things get better with your life, though, and that you can find other healthy outlets on which to place your heavy emotional burdens. I know we thought we'd be in each other's lives forever. Maybe we will be. But probably not in the way we imagined. If you ever come across this, feel free to find me and talk to me about it. It may be a sign that we should actually talk it out, which we still might. But right now it seems best to let things fade as they have been.

Sincerely,
Benjamin

· ·

Dear you,

We have been friends for many years, and during those years we have had many ups and downs, but through it all we had still remained good friends. Recently, many things have happened, most of them not so good. Even though I have had my selfish moments and haven't always been there for you, it was a tough time, and I wanted to be there for you aside from all that has happened in the past. You moved to a new town hours away from your family and friends. I tried several times to meet up with you to hang out, but you said you didn't want to hang out with anyone, only to find out you wanted to hang out with someone just the next day. I let it go, hoping you would get in touch with me to hang out. Later on, you wrote me, just saying hi. I wrote back that same day and logged on almost every day for a week, hoping to find a response from you, but I found nothing. On that last day I logged on to find you writing to a mutual friend asking if they were staying in town because everyone you knew was going to be gone for the summer. I will still be here. It pains me so much to see that I am not everyone you know. I thought about it that whole day because it bothered me so much. Even through it all, I value our friendship so much that I haven't been able to let go…until now. I can't keep putting myself through this pain when it is obvious you have already given up on me. I can't keep caring about this when I am the only one invested in this friendship. Good luck in all you do.

Sincerely,
me

Dear old friend,

First of all, I want to let you know that I really miss you. I think about you every day, and my mind runs around in circles—happy thoughts, sad thoughts, guilt. I really wish I had told you everything you meant to me, because you had such an impact on my life. You inspired me to be the best person I could be, to always be happy, to live a life for others, and to be brave. You were a better person than I'll ever be, and you touched so many people's lives.

I keep thinking about that haunting dream I had a few weeks after your funeral, how in my dream we were all at your funeral again, and you were sitting right next to me. And how we were all joking around and laughing like we did in the old days, and I knew I wasn't just seeing things because everyone else saw you too. And how suddenly you realized whose funeral it was, and you started crying, and we all started crying too. And how suddenly the organist started playing Nocturne in E Flat Major, and you disappeared, and we were all that was left, sitting at your funeral, broken, listening to Chopin. And how for days afterward I didn't believe that you were actually gone.

I listen to songs that make me think of you, and I remember the happy times to make myself laugh, and I do all this just so I don't feel guilty that I never said goodbye, never knew you were sick until the day you passed away. I think of the last time I saw you, how I hadn't seen you in two years, how we hugged and hugged, and I pretend that the hug was a goodbye, an "I love you". Maybe it was, but at the time, I thought it was "hello again". I wasn't ready for goodbye. If I was, maybe I would have been better about keeping in touch. I've always been horrible about calling people, but I still have your old number in my phone, a memory of all the times I could have called but didn't. I'm sorry for that. Remember the day you came over and decided that you should turn my treadmill on its highest speed and jump on it? And how you flew into the couch and landed in a heap and even though I'm sure it hurt, you were in hysterics. Come to think of it, everyone else was, too. But we were all too scared to try it for ourselves. I was too scared to try a lot of things that came naturally to you. Your open heart, the way you let everyone in—no wonder you had so many friends. Turns out, I don't have a heart like that. My heart is afraid of breaking, like it did when you left. My heart is afraid of aching and pulsing and feeling like it's going to burst, like it does now. It's tired of feeling like someone scrubbed it with a Brillo pad until it was raw and vulnerable. It wants to feel good again.

Maybe my heart would feel good again if I could go back in time and be closer to you. Maybe it wouldn't hurt so much if I had called you and kept in touch. Maybe it would feel okay if I knew that I had been the best friend I could. Maybe it would calm down if only I could remember whether I told you I loved you when I saw you last. Telling you I love you now doesn't cut it. Visiting your grave and hanging your picture in my room won't mend my heart. Maybe it's a reminder to remember what I have, to be grateful, and to hang on to it for dear life. Maybe my heart isn't meant to heal, so I'll never forget my lesson learned in How to Be a Friend. But why did it have to be such a difficult lesson to learn?

I love you, always have. Always will.
Love,
Me

Dear Holly,

You're new to me. I've never talked to you or about you before today, but I think you're absolutely amazing. You're absolutely everything I've ever wanted myself to be. You're confident and beautiful, full of life and laughter. I am so jealous of you.

I was always the shy girl in school, the cute one, the one with the sweet smile, the quiet child. I have always hated that girl for as long as I can remember. I hated the way she talked, the way she grew her hair out long because that's how everyone liked it, the way she cried when she got her first F. I have an anxiety disorder. I have panic attacks, and normal activities like hanging out with friends is too tiring. When I started working, it was a constant struggle just to move my legs back into the grocery store I cashiered at.

I hated me.

And then I chopped all of that hair off, every last strand cropped to my chin, and I met you.

You're so amazing, Holly. You openly dream about being a burlesque dancer, think that stripping your way through college is somehow glamorous in the trashiest way possible, and you actually want to share a mattress in a shitty apartment with three of your friends while you just make art for the rest of your life. You'd rather the roomful of acquaintances than the one best friend because every acquaintance is automatically your best friend, anyway. You want entire sleeves of tattoos, and you wear black nail polish to hide the grime under your nails. You drink and curse and smoke. You dance. God, watching you dance is like having a full-on religious experience for me.

Holly, you're everything I've only ever dreamed of being. I'm so jealous of you.

You told me that you liked my hair, seemed really sincere in that calm, almost eerie way you sometimes are when you say something you really believe in, and I trembled.

A lot of people don't like you. A lot of people think you're selfish. They prefer me, they say, because I'm 'real'. They think that you're too much, and you are. But for someone like me, someone who was nothing at all before I met you, you will always be just enough.

Valerie

Dear You,
I can't be just your friend. It hurts too much. I'm sorry, but either I mean everything to you or nothing at all. I can't stand this in-between crap.
Sincerely,
Me

Dear D.J.

    I will never see the Jewelry Channel on the TV without thinking of you. I will never hear the roar of an Acura Integra without thinking of you driving down my street. I will never be able to not think about you on the first day of school. I will never forget the moment we almost kissed in my driveway. I will never be able to see or smell Michael Jordan cologne without smelling you. I will never be able to hear the music of Eminem without thinking how you impersonated him in Middle School. I will never be able to grasp how my eleven year old nephew is so much like you and at the age when you and I first kissed and started "going out" – whatever that meant to eleven year olds. I will never forget the roar of your motorcycle, the way your mom loved me, the day your baby siblings truly remembered me when I walked in and ran into my arms and I will never forget the times when it was just you and I and you were … you.

    You still call and I still answer, but I wonder if you realize the amount of disappointment in my voice when I say hello and goodbye. Everything about your life right now disappoints me. I told you how I felt about you all those years ago on my Birthday, which, let me just say now, you are infamous for ruining Birthdays. Remember when you dropped out of high school on my Birthday?? Yeah, I do. Your life, if you can call it that, makes me sad. I grew up with someone who I thought could do anything. Your dad was a firefighter, you lived in a dream home with a wonderful mother who would do anything for you and you let all of us down.

    Does the mom you rely on so much know that you do drugs? Does the father who you used to be a junior firefighter with know that you wake up and immediately smoke a bowl? Do your little brother and sister know that you can't go one night without drinking? Does that ONE girl who I know you loved know how you ended up? If she did, do you think she would be proud of you? The only people who are proud of you are the people who you surround yourself with now and that's not saying much.

    If there's one thing I regret it would be not telling you that I loved you that one moment in my driveway when we almost kissed. That was my chance, and I blew it. I know you'd be everything I knew you could be if you were with me. I know you'd be the D.J. I saw so much potential in; the D.J. who would run to my house when we were kids just to sit on my porch; the D.J. who I went to Hebrew class with, not because I'm Jewish, too, but just to be with you that much longer; the D.J. who had passion about something more important than drugs, alcohol and slutty girls.

    I hoped you would find out one day how well I treated you and maybe, just maybe, realize that I could give you the world. What was I to you? I guess I expected more out of someone who would only show me disappointment for years to come. One day I might come back to you. Maybe one day you'll be the person I want to be proud of, but, for now, I'm really disappointed in you.

With hope,
The best friend you've ever had.

Dear You,
I didn't appreciate you enough while you were still with me and for that, I often hate myself.
I miss you so very much. I still weep for you - on your birthday, the day you died, when a sad movie reminds me of you, when your great-granddaughter wears one of your expressions.
I miss you so very much it's hard to breathe when I think of you. Your voice, your face, reaches out to me in my mind. I can almost grab them and hold them in my heart but then they evaporate in the mist.
I want to make things up to you, the times I wasn't there for you, the times we fought, the times I took you for granted, but how can I? You're not here. You're in heaven.
I feel you watching over me, whether or not I deserve it, and I'm grateful and feel blessed, if undeserving. I wish you could have met all your grandchildren, that you could have seen them grow up, that you could have seen your great-grandchildren.
Your granddaughter is everything to me that I should have been to you and wasn't. You doted on me, and I pulled back. I didn't realize the treasure I had until you were far away and dying, and then gone.
I hope you will forgive me.
I hope you still love me.
I hope I will see you again.
I will always and forever love you.

■■

Dear blameless,
If I had the guts to scream these things in your face, then I would. If I did scream at you, that would only bring me down to your level. Being on your level means de-friending people on Facebook, so they can't see your pathetic statuses because you are too passive aggressive to face them, using Twitter to tell people about people you hate, pushing the blame off on anyone else but yourself, trying to create sides with friend groups, playing the victim, using excuses, and just being crazy in general.
I am not going to take back that this problem began and needs to end with you. You screwed up, and you will not admit it. I apologized for being mean to you, because apparently you cannot take some heated criticism. You are going to be a terrible politician then. God, I hope you never run for office. You'll be crying every day if you cried from a few e-mails that hurt your feelings. I actually enjoyed saying those mean things to you.
I'm going to act like everything is fine starting tomorrow, but really it's not. I now look at you as less of a person. I wish you didn't live with me. I was praying that you decided to move elsewhere. I will be nice to you because I am the bigger person, and I never want to be on such a petty level that you have put yourself and your drama on. You asked for respect so I am going to give it you, not because I think you deserve it, but because I realize that it will make life much easier. I know that I'm being overdramatic right now, but I think you suck as a person. I do not care that the whole world is out to get you. I do not care about your excuses. And I especially do not care if you like me.
Glad that is settled,
Me

Dear T,

I remember the day when we first hung out. I fell for you instantly; you were different from anyone I had ever met. You were genuinely great.

I remember when you first kissed me. It was like magic. I can't describe how perfect it seemed to me - how perfect YOU seemed to me.

I remember you telling me that if we would break up, you would want to remain friends because you think I'm cool. I felt the same.

I remember the day I shared my biggest secret with you, the one thing that's always been heavy in my heart. I remember you confiding in me as well and being patient with me as I sat there crying in your car for so long.

I remember the day I waved at you from across the street, and you didn't wave back. You were scared. You had been thinking some things over. You broke my heart.

I remember walking away without saying goodbye. I went for a walk. It was cloudy, but I wore my sunglasses so no one would see me cry. I especially didn't want you to see me cry. I wanted you to think I was strong.

I remember barely being able to smile for days, crying in my room for weeks and missing you for months.

T, you were my first real friend in a new town. You helped me make friends, you made me feel at home, you saved me from the misery I was feeling, you protected me when I was in trouble, you shared my heaviest burdens with me, and you reintroduced me to God. Sometimes I regret dating you because it so very much changed all these things. It changed our friendship, the way we talk to each other, and the way I feel about myself.

For the longest time I thought there must be something wrong with me, and I thought you must be too perfect to be with someone like me. But I realize that was a mistake. I realized it when weeks later I told you I wanted a hug, and you picked me up and held me tight like you used to. It was then that I really realized I couldn't be mad at you. I couldn't hate you, because I needed you. I still need you. I just don't know how to tell you.

T, your friendship meant so much to me, and now that it's hanging on by a thread, my heart cannot stop aching. You've done so much for me, T. I need you to be there to do more.

I need you to be my friend, and I hope so much that you value me enough to need me to be yours. I don't want to have to miss you anymore.

Sincerely,
Your Old Friend

••

Dear Greg,
I wish I could tell you my deepest secret. You called me fat the day I was diagnosed with bulimia. I have bulimia because I want to be thin enough for you to love me the way I love you. You're my best friend, but that will never be enough for me.

Dear B,

I just want to thank you for everything. You have no idea how much you absolutely mean to me, and without you, I don't think I'd even be alive to this day. You've saved my life more than once, you've made me carry on and live, and I don't regret it at all. Thank you for the extra year and a half your words have given me.

But today, it just feels like it can't go on anymore. I thought I was doing so much better, but I'm really not. I'm so sick and tired of faking every waking moment of my life, from looking interested in classes, to "laughing" at people's stories and jokes. I hate it. I hate myself for lying to them, to me, to the world.

I'll never be who I want, and that just makes me so insanely angry. Every time I'm about to just blow up, and let everything out, all my tears and fears and everything...I immediately put up this wall, that just keeps everything inside. Even though I'm all alone, I still won't let myself break down. What if it all explodes one day? I think it's already starting to...

I don't want to be another stupid teenage cliché. I think it's a bit late for that. I'm really sorry for being so stupid and hypocritical and selfish. But once I'm gone, you won't need to deal with me anymore. It's really just better for the world in the end.

I just want you to know that you're the closest friend I've ever had, and you mean the most to me. More than Sam, more than my family, more than anyone. just, thanks. For everything.

I'm really sorry.

-L

Dear Boy,

You probably don't know this but that night you called me 5 years ago I had a gun in hand ready to kill myself. You told me you loved me and that I meant a lot to you. Thank you for saving my life even though you didn't know you did.

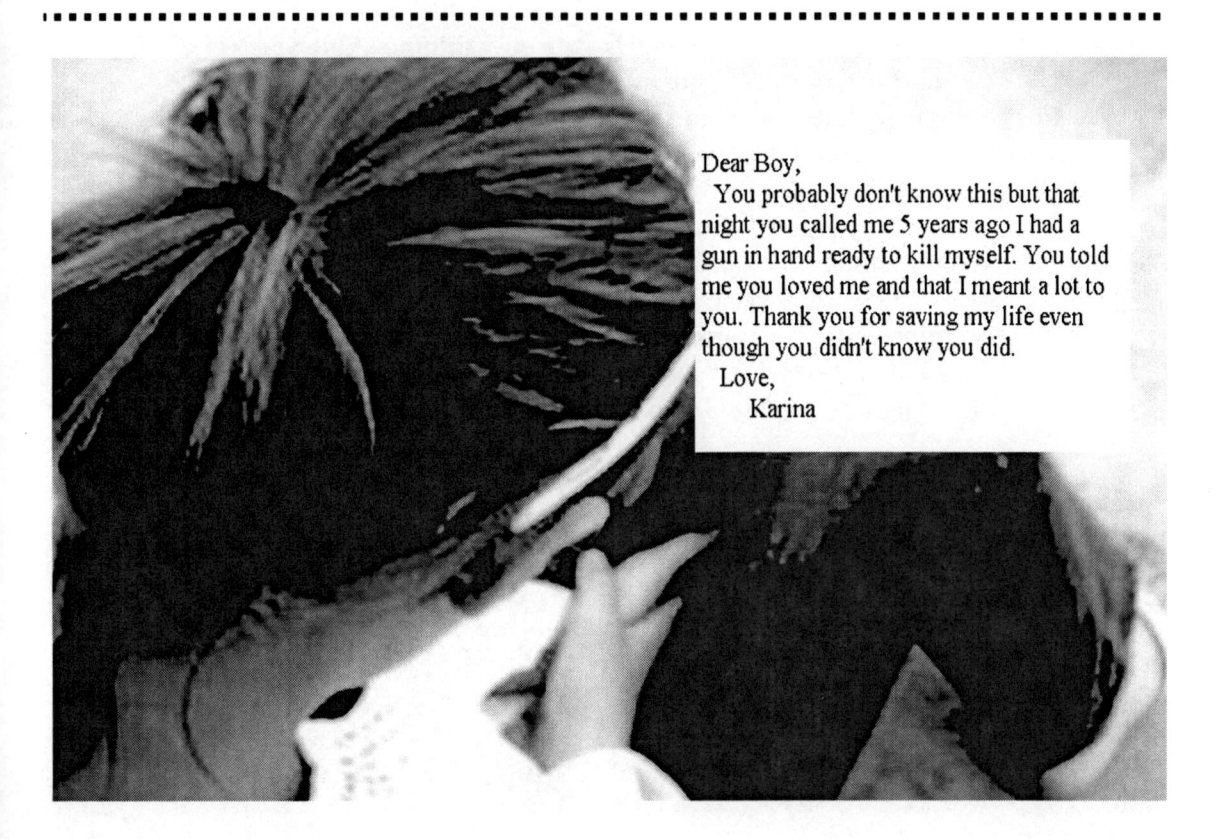

Love,
Karina

Dear Self,

Since you can't seem to take your own advice, I thought maybe I could inspire you with the opposite of your own advice. Read this, and think about it carefully.

The Grand List of Post-Breakup Anti-Advice

1. Assume that when you haven't heard from friends in a while, it's because they don't want to have anything to do with you.
2. Don't give him time, your needs are more urgent!
3. You can do it all on your own, don't let others see you weak.
4. Don't tell your love how you really feel because of what other people will think and say about you.
5. Do anything to alleviate your pain when you're miserable, regardless of its effects on others.
6. Distance yourself, and protect your heart.
7. Gossip all you want in order to feel better about yourself.
8. Alienate others as "weird" so that you don't have to deal with them and so you feel you have social authority.
9. Act on your hormones when they're the only thing making you feel good about yourself.
10. Cry alone in your room, and don't ask for help -- it is okay to wallow in your misery. As a matter of fact, send everyone an angsty Facebook message while you're at it.
11. Run away from and ignore your pain.
12. Convince yourself that you've been abandoned and that no one is obligated to care about you anymore.
13. Dress really grungy to match your outside with what you feel on the inside.
14. Be awkward around your ex every time you see him.
15. Whatever you do, DO NOT discuss the breakup with him.

There. Think about it. Then decide what how you want to act.

Sincerely,
Yourself

Me, Myself and my Alter ego

Alter ego is a great thing. It is neither some attribute that villains in thrillers adorn nor it is a disorder that Hollywood personifies. It is simply the other-side of you that wants to emerge. We all have alter egos. What I initially thought as a total transformation was in fact just my alter ego popping out to take a lungful of fresh air. And I think it's simply a reaction from our body to high stress. My alter ego had done the exact thing it was designed to do – relieve stress and regain focus.

I was having a great summer – had spent the best part of it with my family and friends. Since I was back to normalcy, it did occur to me that I did not have two important things – an internship and money. But my response to it, a learned one, was "So what?" All of a sudden, I was beginning to enjoy little things life threw at me – tennis games with my uncle, jogs in the great Golden Gate Park, working out, eating at restaurants, watching movies, talking to friends and meeting new people. And boy, did I meet some wonderful people!

And when one close friend left, another filled in right away. It is amazing how good friends can pick up from where you last left, anytime, anyplace – simply phenomenal.

Dear my evil twin (my sinful self),

    I no longer wish to be around you anymore. I keep trying to reject you, but no matter how hard I try you always keep coming back. Why can't you just leave me alone for good? I don't want to have anything to do with you. Whenever you are around people get hurt; others as well as me. The only ones who ever get any fun out of it are yourself, your evil friends, and your master (your driving force). I have my own friends now, my own life now, and I no longer want to be in your presence; nor you in mine. You mask yourself by telling me that you're just my human nature, but my human nature is not to hurt others, not to feel guilty for what I've done, not to cry myself to sleep at night because I can't stand the fact of trying to live another day with you. What I really want to know is how you can even enjoy yourself and live with yourself.
    But now that I think about it all you really do is create all the damage without my knowledge and leave the mess for me to clean up. But whatever you do, do not try to get a hold of my friends.
    They have enough to bear. I could not stand the fact of how devastated they would be if they found out who you truly were. So I am making a proposal, when I finish this letter, you go your way without me, and I will go my way (heart and soul).

Dear Future Me,

You obviously know that you have embarked on a bigger journey than ever before. You are far from home. You can't rely on English to get by. This is not your comfort zone.

By now you can look back at your old self. I don't have to tell you about how I am feeling, but I will anyway, in the case that you forgot (which is the goal). You are lonely and wishing time would go by faster. You are slowly making new friends but struggling to keep them from straying to other groups. You have so much to offer; one of these days you'll find someone who realizes that. I hope that you, future self, can look back and laugh at this silly statement as you relax with your new friends.

You're scared. Terrible things happen in places like these, and you don't want to be a victim. You're struggling to fit in culturally and socially. You're plagued by the guilt from coming on this expensive and prolonged trip.

Is there light at the end of the tunnel? There's no way of knowing. But I hope that you, future self, have benefited from this experience. You're a creature of habit, and you wallow in your sadness. I long to break out, and I hope that by the time this reaches you that you are finally happy like you've always imagined.

Love, Old Self

•••

Hello. This is the present. I'm not sure what you're trying to hint at. I'm unsure of which direction to take. If you could, please send me a definite sign. Thanks,

My best,

Me -- as I am, right at this moment – waiting

•••

Dear Me,

I miss you. What happened to you? Where did you go? You used to be so full of life and energy. Remember all those goals, plans, and ideas. You were going to take over the world. You were going somewhere. You were going to be a somebody. And now, you seemed to have forgotten what it is that makes you- you. What happened to all your spunk and pizzazz? You've lost all your inspiration and motivation. I know deep down you know this is true. And I know it's still in you, somewhere. So dig deep- reach in- and pull it out. The world is waiting. I am waiting. I need you. I miss you. Please, come back to me. Soon.

Love,
Me

Dear Alcoholic,

I needed you. I was under your spell. It started out just a few drinks on the weekends, then a few drinks turned into blackouts. Day-drinking. Skipping class to drink. I stopped caring about my appearance. I didn't shower for days. I couldn't get out of bed. The only reason I did get out of bed was to drink. Underage drinking, might I add.

I never did drink every day, so why would anyone label me an alcoholic? "I'm just a normal college kid having fun." But do "normal" college kids skip class, blow off tests, and stop eating because alcohol replaces food? I guess not.

Bipolar. Depression. Me. I was drinking my pain away. So far away from home. I just wanted to feel numb, I guess. I felt there was no out. And there was no way I was going to stop drinking.

Today, I am 4 months sober. It's been a tough journey to sobriety. Believe me, I never thought I could give up something that I had been doing since freshman year of High School.

I am a different person today. I know who I am. I know where I belong in this world. I'm, dare I say, happy. What the heck, I feel GREAT! "One day at time." The AA motto. I can't predict the future, all I can do is take it "one day at a time" to conquer my addiction.

Today, I am proud to say that my name is Sarah, and I'm an Alcoholic. I wouldn't give back these 4 months for anything.

Thank you for this second chance at life.
Love,
Me

Dear Brandon,

I just got it. It was like you walked up and handed me the answer I was looking for. I know why God put you in my life and then took you away.

I never loved anyone the way I loved you. If I hadn't known that kind of love, I never would have known that even one day wasted is too much. I have spent almost a year questioning God and why he took you from me, and now I know.

I do not want a single day to go by without the people I still have here knowing how much I love and adore them.

I let you go without a fight, because I was too scared to say that I love you. I can't, I won't, I refuse to ever let that happen again.

There will never be another you. There will never be anyone to replace you or repair my heart. But, there are still plenty of people in front of me that I don't express my feelings for. I'm not looking for love, that kind of love only comes around once. You will always be the only one. But, now I know that I have to appreciate and embrace everything that is still here. Thank you for helping me finally get it.

I love you always and miss you eternally,
Broken

Dear Joshua,

You are the love of my life. We met in high school when I was only fourteen years old. I was searching for love but didn't find it in you for two more years. We got together as a fling, nothing serious; no strings attached. My heart was hooked, but I would never tell. Two and a half years later, we are broken up. My decision. Wrong. We fought way too much, and I thought it would do us good. I thought we could take some time, move on, live apart to see how it worked. We both had new people way too soon. Place-holders that would keep our minds busy. It didn't work. As much as I may try, my mind always goes back to you. A certain smell, a certain memory brings me back to everything we had. When I decided to take time in the relationship, I could only focus on the fighting. Now that I have taken time, I can see everything as it was. Love. We did fight; too much, but it meant something. It was full of passion and hope. Our love was something different; unique. No one could ever feel the same as we did. I have had enough time. I'm ready. And although I wish this statement would be enough to bring you back to me, it hasn't proven to be. I know you are hurt and confused and that you need more time, but I will continue to wait. Although you tell me to move on, my future lies with you. I can still feel your kisses and can see every lash that touches your gorgeous green eyes. My heart is with you, mo matter where you are in life. Come back to me, love. So we can continue on our journey together and not waste any more time.

I love you Joshua.

Love, Jessica

Hey there Superman...

We just got off the phone, and I'm already missing you, though I won't say so. I've been hurt too much, learned not to trust... I know you say you are falling for me, that you want to be with me, and as much as it should worry me considering the short amount of time we've been talking, it doesn't.

I'm excited, nervous, and perhaps falling a bit as well. I won't tell you though, I have to hold onto myself somehow. I can't fall too far too fast, or at least... can't let you know how far or fast. Just in case it doesn't go well next weekend when I see you.

If we end up not having this amazing chemistry in person, then I can walk away without you knowing how disappointed and upset I might be. You'll never know how close I came to taking such a big risk of getting involved with a virtual stranger.

I would take the risk, too. If the chemistry is there. If we are as comfortable and content in person as we are online/text/phone lately. If it feels as natural and right to be in your arms as I hope it will. I'm willing to take all of those risks, because we have so many mutual friends that it's amazing we haven't met sooner. Because someone that we both trust, who knows us both incredibly well, says it might be exactly what we both need.

I want it. Want it all so badly that my dreams are full of your voice, your smile, and hopes for the future. I'm not a white picket fence kind of girl, but I dream about waking up beside you every morning for a year. Ten years... Curling up on the couch together to watch a movie. Taking walks, going grocery shopping, cooking dinner together.

And yes... those things that you say to me on the phone, when your voice deepens just a little bit more and you almost seem to growl just a bit. The things that make me shiver and pine for you, that make me impatient to see you and find out if this chemistry will still exist.

That is the roadblock. The hurdle. I will not promise anything until we are standing face to face, until we know whether there is still potential or just disappointment that the other didn't measure up somehow. I cannot tell you any of these thoughts until after I know whether it is safe to move forward, safe to dream...

I don't look at this as an Internet thing, since we have so many of the same friends and have been running in the same circles... I just think of it as irony that it took so long for us to actually be in the same place at the same time.

I will tell you here, where maybe it'll get posted and maybe in two weeks I will bring up the page for you to read... I am falling, just a bit. I feel it, I know it. I could fall completely if I were not deliberately holding myself back. I WANT to fall.

I preferred the song Wicked Game when I misheard the lyric as "I wanna fall in love with you" instead of 'I don't want'. I thought the song had such yearning, such passion, falling for someone in spite of not wanting to. If that were the lyric, it would be my song for you.

Please be the man I think you are, so that you can read this one day.
Yours?
"Sally"

Hey Superman...

I wrote a letter here a couple of months ago, but it never got published. It was intense, full of how scared I was of meeting you in person for the first time and how excited I was at the idea of all those words becoming reality.

It still hasn't happened, and though I still hope for it and accept your excuses to cancel every opportunity to make the 4-hour drive... I move through my days heartbroken and lost, wishing I could still cling to the dream of all those wonderful things you used to say.

I've been distant lately, claiming it's because I know you have things going on that you need to focus on... but really I'm just waiting for you to call me again, or at least text, or respond to one of my IMs or Facebook comments. Waiting, but not surprised when it doesn't happen.

I miss you, the idea of what might have been, and all of those fantasies you poured into my head. My heart aches with the certainty that the moment passed before we could grab onto it and the fear that you never meant any of it in the first place.

Finding you saved me from a dark place within myself, lifted me up and gave me hope for a while. Each day that passes without contact or response, I slip backward a bit. Any day now I'll wake up and be that broken girl again, the one you promised to save, and it'll be too late even if you did mean what you said.

I meant it when I said you were my last chance, that if this didn't work out I'd give up.

The thought that it might have all been a game or a brief distraction for you, it destroys me inside. More devastating than anything else I've suffered through, more hurtful than any of the things that my abusive ex(s) put me through.

In giving me hope and then taking it away you've hurt me more than they ever could have, more cruel than any sadistic punishment I've experienced.

If none of it was real, I don't think I'll ever be able to forgive myself for having fallen for you.

Please come back and tell me this is all paranoia, a silly girl afraid of being hurt by yet another boy, terrified of trusting when it's been betrayed by so many others. You don't have to love me, just be my friend. You don't even have to do that, if you've lost interest, just promise it wasn't a game you were playing.

I've suffered and survived a LOT, but I don't know if I can make it through that. If it was never real, I don't think I can handle that.

Please...

Hey Superman...

I've spent the last 24 hours in misery and confusion, trying to figure out what is wrong with me that I keep getting into situations with men like you. Men who claim to care for me, even say they love me, say they want to be with me, build these beautiful dreams of the life that we could share... then out of nowhere they start dating someone else. I posted here when I first started falling... I posted again when I was fairly sure it was all a mind game on your part and hoped I was wrong. I figure I may as well post this last time, close the story as it were, and say goodbye.

I still care for you. I could have loved you in that way that you say you can't live without. I would have loved you so much that you'd never have spent a moment in doubt of my devotion, and all I'd have asked for is that you let me, and keep me in your life, and love me at least a little in return. In my way, I do love you that way a bit, and maybe the story isn't over yet.

If it doesn't work out with whoever she is (and I hope for your sake that it does, you deserve someone who will make you happy), I'll probably still be around. In my life thus far, I've never really stopped caring for anyone that I once loved, and this thing that we nearly had... there was so much damn potential for it to be a great and wonderful thing for both of us...

If you come back in a few months, in a year, or later... If I'm available, chances are I'll be willing to give it another try.

Right now I'm a little heartbroken, but it's more the idea of what could've been that I'm mourning. I still count you as a friend and still want you in my life as a friend, so I don't mourn the loss of you. Just those beautiful dreams that you built for us being together, the wonderful things that you used to say.

I pine for those dreams, and hope that we'll both get to live them someday. If not together then with someone who is as good for us as we each fully deserve.

The main thing I'm really upset at you for right now is not being up front with me. I gave you every opportunity to let me know you had lost interest, that you found someone local that you wanted.. I asked you, if that should happen, to please just tell me bluntly, so I wouldn't have to spend weeks of confusion and misery trying to figure out why I'm being ignored or avoided. You promised to do that, but you didn't. You also promised you wouldn't throw me away for someone local, but I never intended to hold you to that. I hope that your breaking the other promise was because you thought somehow it would be easier having both broken, though you'd be wrong.

No, there's something else I'm upset about actually. On top of not letting me know that you'd lost interest, or found someone closer... I had to find out from the Facebook notification that listed you as now being 'in a relationship'. That hurt. Gods it hurt so much. I just wanted to curl up in a ball and sob. That broke my heart far more painfully and thoroughly than just telling me you'd found someone else would've done.

If you ever do come back, and I say no, it will likely be because of that cruelty. I may not be able to trust you again, when you've broken the only promise I ever asked you for.

Dear EB,

You are making me so angry right now! Quit thinking you have it all figured out. Quit being so high-and-mighty! So what if you were a Resident Assistant in college and learned all these "amazing things" about life! So what if you come from humble beginnings, so what if you have Daddy issues? Stop trying to be an expert on my life! You're not me!

Quit telling me things about myself that I either want to forget about or already know. What's the point? I'm very well aware that I'm too hard on myself. I'm very well aware that I fear failure. But what is this going to solve? What is this even going to help? I'll just feel worse about myself if you pick apart my shortcomings. It's not helping me get over them; it's just putting them in the limelight. "Here everybody, let's all look at Holly's issues and make her even more embarrassed about them!" Or worse -- "You know, Holly, you should embrace your shortcomings! Celebrate them! That's what everyone else does! Hooray for failure!"

Maybe I should just move on and not talk to you for a while. We shouldn't have dated, that's for sure. Especially not when I was still heart-broken over Mark.

Just give me some space,
Holly

Dear MT,

I might be in love with you. You're not up to society's standards of good-looking, and your hairdo came out of a magazine from the 90s, but... I don't really care. Your personality caused me to take a second look and a third. It was then that I noticed how tall you are. Your smile. The facial expressions you made around me but not around others. Our conversations and your sincerity caused me to look again and notice the way you would stop on your way to accomplish something and make time to joke around with me or ask me how my day was going, ... and I noticed the shape of your shoulders and back when you'd lean with one arm on the doorway, talking to someone else about some important business matter. I continued typing away at my computer. But I took note of these things.

You're older than me by half a decade. And we would get so much crap if people even knew that we talked outside the office. Unless, of course, we finally just left that office. Easier said than done in this economy though, I suppose. Let's keep up this not-really-inappropriate-but-possibly-frowned-upon correspondence. Okay?

Sincerely,
SB

Dear Boy,
We've become incredibly close friends. I'd consider you to be one of the best ones I've been graced with in a long time. I know that you're falling in love with me. I can see it a little more every time I see you. I love you too.
However, you are 32, I am 18. You are a boy; I have lived my life as a lesbian for the past 8 years. You are staying here; I am being deployed in 2.5 months. I told you today that I want to just start acting on my desires, and it's true.
The problem is I don't know how to respond to you.
Tomorrow night, please just kiss me.
Truly yours,
Lolita

••

Dear Zac,
I love you too.
Love,
Annaliese

Dear Matt,

If you ever read this you'd probably be scared that I'd tell you I like you again. Let's not kid ourselves, I'll never stop. Matt, what I'm writing to tell you is that of your divine potential. Matt, I can see deep inside you, and I can tell you will be a great man one day but only if you grow up. Matt, you've been putting off your mission, and I'm hugely scared that you won't go. You need this Matt. You need to get out of your hometown and see the world and have people depend on you. Matt, the reason I've liked you throughout the years is because I can see the greatness in you. I am often disgusted by the ways you act now, but when you eventually grow up you'll be the greatest man in the world. I know it's hard to hear, but someone needs to say it. That night you met my parents you were wholly the man that I love. That night was a shining moment to me because after you left both of my parents said they approved of you. They saw the man you were portraying, and they loved him. Matt, when you become that man I will love you so much more. Matt, you're my best friend. We've stuck together for 5 of the hardest years either of us have ever had. We've seen friends fall away and leave, yet you and I are still stuck together. That's why I love you now, but you'll become so much better when you grow up. All those girls you kiss and the one you date are not what you need. You need someone who challenges you and you know that I do. I know it's distant and a bit odd, but if you ever do grow up, I want to marry you. And if you never do grow up, I want to marry a man who has the qualities that you could have. Matt, know that this is not for me. Growing up would do you a world of good. I hope at some point that you do. If or when you do go on a mission and you come back and you still don't want to marry me, well then I'll be fine with that. To know that you became who I knew you could be will be good enough for me. I love you Matt. I always will.

Love with all my heart,
Amanda

To you,

To write this letter is to admit the wrong you did to me. It seems unreal to actually think I knew you – who you were, what mattered to you. You aren't who I thought you were at all. And it hurts me every time I see you. It's like that nervous feeling when your stomach gets all in knots, and you can't breathe. And I hate it. You were one of my best friends, and I trusted you. You took advantage of that trust more than I can ever explain. You made me feel like less of a woman because you thought since I was drunk you could do whatever you wanted to me. Just know that it's not okay, and it never will be. I trusted you with my life and my friendship. You made me feel stupid for giving that to you. No one knows about what you did, because it hurts me to think about it, to speak about it, to admit that it's real. But it is real, and I need to face that. You took advantage of me. Most people may think I should never forgive you, because you're messed up, with no morals or value of friendship and trust. But in addition to forgiving you, I'll pray for you. I hope that you figure out what is truly important in life and never make another person feel the way you made me feel. I hope you turn out okay, and I hope that I forget.

-Anonymous

Dear Boyfriend,
Thank you so much for being so caring and gentle with me. You have no idea how much it means to me to have you. After my last boyfriend and all his passion, it is such a relief to be able to actually watch a movie.
Love,
Me

YOU….

From the first day I saw YOU, when I look at YOU my heart skips a beat
When YOU'RE with me nothing else seems to matter
When YOU call me "YOUR girl" I feel like the luckiest girl in the world
I can't imagine my life without YOU in it
There's not a day that goes by without there being thoughts of YOU running through my mind
When YOU touch me I get Goosebumps
YOU can make me laugh like no one else can
YOU can turn my tears into a smile
YOU are truly a beautiful person inside and out
Days spent with YOU feel like seconds
When I'm in YOUR arms I feel like nothing can go wrong
It makes me feel special when YOU catch my eye across a crowded room

……….I wish YOU knew how much YOU meant to me

Dear Friend,

I don't really know how to start a letter like this.

It has been about a month since we talked, and I know it sounds childish, but I am just now figuring out how I feel about everything that you told me. What I said before, about you and your newly expected bundle of joy, is true. I am so happy for you. I still believe that you are going to be an amazing mom, even if that's not how you planned for things to go.

But this month has helped me figure out some of the other emotions that cropped up in that span of five minutes that we got to talk. And as selfish as this might sound, I am mad at you. I am mad that your child is also his child and not mine. I am mad that you couldn't wait for me to come along and finally sweep you off of your feet like I always dreamed of doing. I know that's irrational and that I never told you how I felt about you. And so, I am mad at me, too. I am mad that I never told you about all the feelings that sat just below the surface for so long, even though you would sit there with me and watch TV for hours on end. I guess it was just that I loved that time I got to spend with you so much that I never wanted to see it slip away. I always assumed that this too would pass and that I would have my chance then. So I guess I am also mad at you for being the sort of friend that I would never want to lose. I realize that this, too, is irrational. All I can say is that I now realize what they mean when they say that love makes you crazy. Because that is the biggest realization I've had over this last month – that I love you. I love every little thing about you, from your smile to your bouts of complete randomness. Inside and out, you are the most beautiful woman that I have ever known.

But I also have come to the understanding that I have to let you go. For someone who uses so many clichés, it seems like painful irony that I would have to live out one of the biggest ones out there – That if you love something, let it go. And if it is meant to be, then it will find its way back to you.

I didn't tell you this, but the day after you told me that you were pregnant, I went out and joined a gym. I guess, deep down, I thought that if I could mold myself into the physically ideal man, I'd have a chance at winning you back. But I've come to realize that I think that is something that I am now doing for someone else. Maybe it's another woman. Maybe it's you. Who knows? But I do know that it is, first and foremost, something that I am doing for me. And so I thank you and your child for that gift. You two were the catalyst I needed in my life, and for that, I am grateful.

The one thing that stays the same is that I will always care about you deeply and will do anything I can to help you. Because in the end, I am still that guy that is scared to death about losing your friendship.

Yours always,
A moment too late.

Dear Boy,

There are so many reasons we can't be together. We really shouldn't. You and one of my good friends almost started a relationship. So, already, that's a major taboo. I'm moving across the country to go to school. That hardly ever works. You're leaving the country after you graduate. What then? But here's what I'm getting at: I don't think any of those things really matter.

We have such a good time. You make me laugh. I make you laugh. We love the same things. We could be together forever and never stop having fun together, never get tired of each other. I believe that, and I think you do too. We get along so well.

There are ways around the things standing in our way. I don't want to let these things get in the way of something that could be really great. We can visit each other at school! Come on, it's not that far, really. I think it could be worth it.

So come on. All I want is to spend more time with you and see what happens. I only have 3 more days with you, and that's just not enough. Are you with me?

Love, Girl

....

Dear Logan,
Why did you have to leave me with this broken heart?

Dear Lover,

It was hard to open my eyes and realize just how much you've hurt me. I promised you death do us part, but I think I will have to go before God and say I can't! I can't end the pain that we cause each other, day in and day out we say nasty spiteful things, and I can't let our daughter grow up like this. I am worried she will grow to hate us both one day! I know that we cannot change the times, and I wouldn't for the life of me go back! Yes I know you would, I know you didn't want to get married or have a child, but you did. All those things you say it kills me because I was truly happy! I was and no I am broken, your words cut me like a knife. If you didn't want to get married, here's your chance to leave, but you still stay! I don't get why, why you put me through this! You say you never do anything wrong, but look at what you've done in the past - you know darn good in well it's abuse. You try to find someone that is to blame for me wanting to leave, and the only person is you! I have for so long made excuses for why you treat me this way, and I am done! I just couldn't see myself without you now I can... And I think I will be happy without you, and even though everything we planned to do together it won't happen the way we wish, we would be unhappy the whole time. Maybe we will go one last time, I can't decide ... I think I just need to move on!
I think you should too!

Dear Abuser,

The intent of our relationship from the beginning was revenge. My heart ached, my soul throbbed, and I simply wanted it to stop. I knew being with you would hurt him … and so it began. I didn't mean to fall so quickly, but I don't feel as if I was in control of that. You are charming, handsome, and smart … everything a woman hopes for in a man. Who knew those bright, blue eyes and dark, curly hair hid a manipulative sense of ownership and jealousy. I consider myself a strong woman. I consider myself to have my best interests in mind. Dating you was not in my best interest. My family hated you, my friends warned me about your actions, but I was blind to all of it. I loved you, you loved me, and that's all there was to it.

I once read a book about a girl in an abusive relationship. I vividly remember reading the words and thinking to myself, "I don't understand how women let that happen!"
Now, I know.
You can't possibly fathom the emotional rollercoaster of an abusive relationship unless you've experienced its turns and drops first hand. The words "I love you" and "I want to spend forever with you" have incredible healing power and the ability to erase any negative action.

At first it was little things, like maybe hitting me a *little* too hard playing "slug bug." And there was your constant verbal abuse … but to the point that I only knew you were cutting me down if I thought about it, so I didn't. You loved me, which was enough. Then came the day when you pushed me down the stairs. In my mind now, sane people would have ended it there … I apparently wasn't sane, because I stayed with you. Truthfully, it's only over because you ended it, and for that, I thank you from the bottom of my heart.

Because of the tremendous emotional pain you caused me, eventually I was able to find myself and move forward with my life. I was able to find the true love of my life and, you don't know this, but we're getting married in September. I've heard you've matured and are dating someone new. I hope she gets the strength to realize that she has incredible self worth without you … just like I did. I forgive you because hatred is a heavy burden to carry, and I still, somehow, believe in the intrinsic good of all people.

Dear Joe,
Our four and half years were absolutely amazing, and I don't regret a single second. I truly love you, and you know that. I don't want you to forget that...but things were just not working. All the fighting and mistrust and deception shouldn't have been there. Things would have only gotten worse, and I wish you the best in everything. I just want you to be happy...

Sincerely,
Breanna.

Dear JT,

I know you were hurt when I ended our relationship and even more so when I told you there would be no chance of us getting back together. I'm sorry I didn't love you like you loved me. But I have to tell you why I can't love you. I have to tell you what made me sick of you.

You made me sad, JT. As I look back on our time together, I realize you were bad for me. You sucked the energy out of me like a black hole. You always came up with some excuse to bring up the horrors of your past relationships - always found a way to beg my sympathy, and I gave it to you. I gave it to you because I was infatuated. Now I realize that you are sad, you are depressing, and you are manipulative. I wish I had realized it sooner. I wish I hadn't said I love you, too, just to avoid hurting your feelings. I wish I hadn't fooled myself into thinking I meant it. I wish I had never dated you.

I'm sorry,
Regretful

Dear My Love,

It has been a pleasure to get to know you, and love you. I must say, I love the time that we spent together. I love your green eyes, your messy light brown hair, and the sweet expression of your face when you smile... I just love you. And I'm not only attracted to you physically, but emotionally and mentally too. The way you project yourself to others, the way you respond, your kindness, and your stubbornness. You're always so friendly, so polite. You never really show that you're mad at someone, but instead you try to remain calm. You're also humble, it is a FACT that you're one of the smartest people your age, but you still deny it and encourage others that they're as smart as you. You're simply a great guy.
But now, I'm feeling like we're slipping apart, fading away along with the wind. Perhaps it's because of your kindness. You care so much about others, that you'd hide your feelings. You'd keep them hidden until it is too late to fix the problems that cause you those uncomfortable feelings. You keep saying that you don't deserve what you have, that you don't deserve all your friends and family. I've always been wondering why you would think so. Why would you think that you're unworthy? That you're selfish? Why can't you see that we're all here for you?
Don't you see me? Can you not trust me? Is it me that caused you to be depressed and fade away? Do you still remember your promise? The only promise that you're so sure you'd keep for all your life?
I'm here for you, and only for you. I've loved you ever since I started to talk to you. I've grown to love you most. Don't you still love me as much as you say you do? You only need to reach out for me, and I'll take your hand.
I can only wish that you read this and figure out that it's me.

Much love,
NN

Dear George,

I can't stop thinking about you. I've known you since the 5th grade, and never in my life would I have guessed that I would have fallen in love with you. YOU were the one that was supposed to fight for me, and here I am fighting for you. You are in my thoughts consistently throughout the day. And when I thought I had cancer, you were the one I called and had YOU check the test results. You are my rock, and I wish that I could be the rock for you, too. I know someday you will realize that I am the one for you. I just hope that it isn't too late. I'm waiting patiently for you. But, patience can only go so far. We are almost 28 years old, and I am ready to start my life with someone. And I hope that person is you. I hope you know that, I know I have said it enough. Please just give me a chance, and I can prove it to you. Thank you for everything that you do for me. I can't wait to kiss those lips, soon.

Love,
Serena

I felt hallow, you made me feel hallow... The scars that run up and down my arm are not there because I want them to be. You made me do it. You took all the love that I had for you and tossed it out the window – sending me into a downward spiral that took me from Heaven to Hell in a matter of seconds. I get it, you don't want me anymore. If only you could see me now bleeding… standing on the edge… would you care enough to stop me from swallowing the bottle of pills? Maybe, maybe not... and even after all this, I still love you.

Loved you once
Love you still
Always have
Aways will

Crystal

Dear Best Friend,
I know that I argue with you a lot, but it's because I love you. Yes I am completely and utterly heartbroken of the fact that you can't see the potential in us. I guess that's what I get when my absolute best friend is a guy. You are my other half, and you have saved my life, although you might not realize that. It just sucks when the whole world, and myself included, thinks that we belong together as more than friends, and you are the only one who doesn't see that. Like in fashion of my favorite movie My Girl, "If you don't get married, will you think and remember me?"
Love with all my heart and then some,
Your Best Friend

Dear friend,

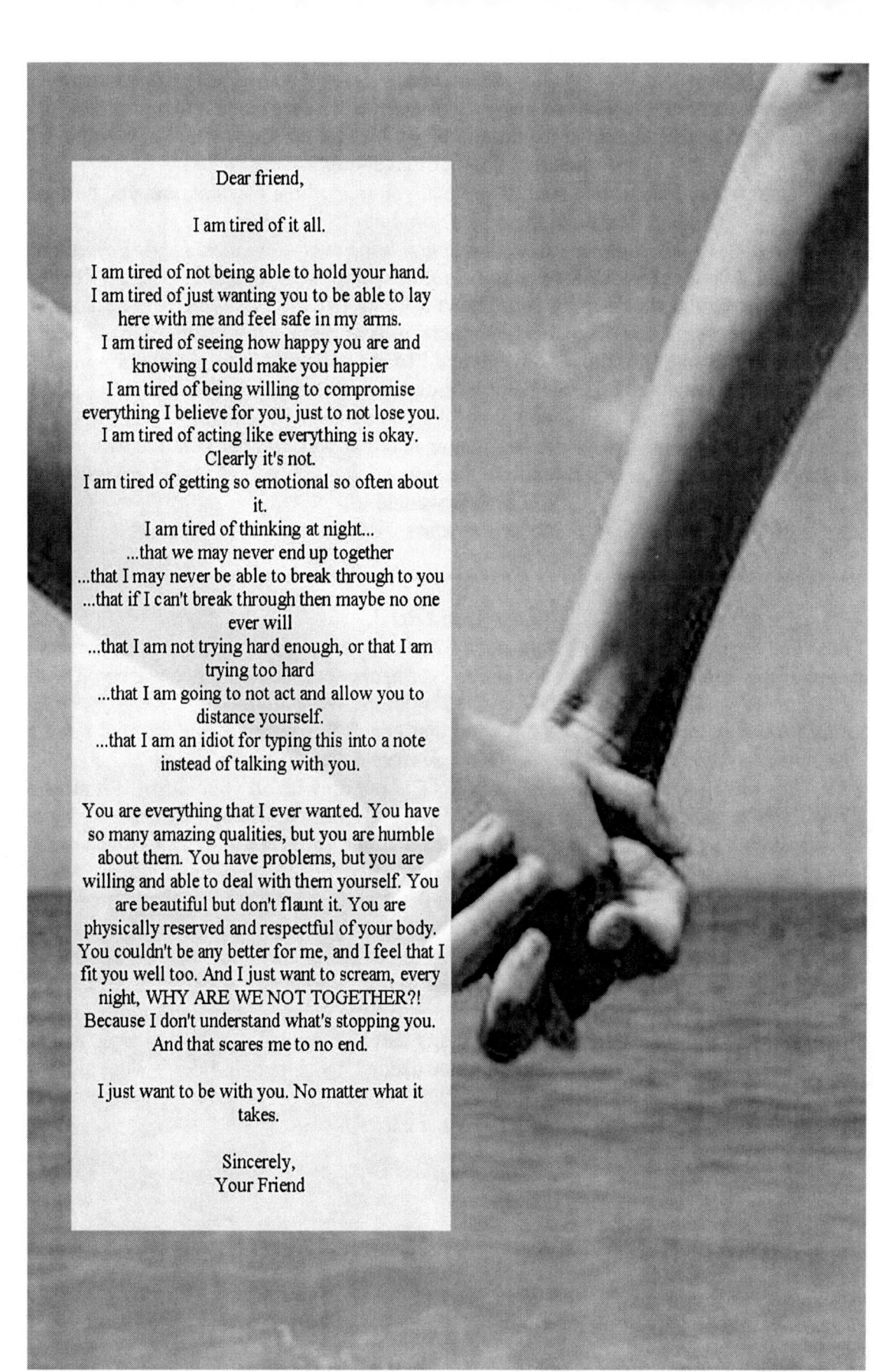

I am tired of it all.

I am tired of not being able to hold your hand.
I am tired of just wanting you to be able to lay here with me and feel safe in my arms.
I am tired of seeing how happy you are and knowing I could make you happier
I am tired of being willing to compromise everything I believe for you, just to not lose you.
I am tired of acting like everything is okay. Clearly it's not.
I am tired of getting so emotional so often about it.
I am tired of thinking at night...
...that we may never end up together
...that I may never be able to break through to you
...that if I can't break through then maybe no one ever will
...that I am not trying hard enough, or that I am trying too hard
...that I am going to not act and allow you to distance yourself.
...that I am an idiot for typing this into a note instead of talking with you.

You are everything that I ever wanted. You have so many amazing qualities, but you are humble about them. You have problems, but you are willing and able to deal with them yourself. You are beautiful but don't flaunt it. You are physically reserved and respectful of your body. You couldn't be any better for me, and I feel that I fit you well too. And I just want to scream, every night, WHY ARE WE NOT TOGETHER?! Because I don't understand what's stopping you. And that scares me to no end.

I just want to be with you. No matter what it takes.

Sincerely,
Your Friend

Dear Oren,

I have written you this letter so many times and yet it never made it to a post box, normally ended up screwed up at the bottom of my bin. I don't know why I never sent it, I thought about it often enough.

I want to thank you. I know that sounds strange, you treated me like shit, and you hurt me so bad. But now, three years on, I am finally over you.

I no longer want to call you every day, I no longer hope every text message or missed call is from you, I no longer wish for you to be online when I sign in, and I no longer check your Bebo account to check up on you. I don't need to. I've forgiven you. And because of that I have moved on and become a better person. And that is why I want to thank you, even though I thought my life was over when I found out you'd been cheating on me. It wasn't. I came through it, and I'm a better person for it. I'm happy in a way that I've never been happy before, I realise now that I don't need you and probably never did.

I really and truly hope that you're happy now and that your life pans out the way you want it to. I pray that you will live life to the full and that you will change the world like you always wanted to.

No longer yours, Nat x

▪▪

Dear Best Friend,

I miss you terribly. It's been 15 days since we parted ways, and I've hated almost every second of it. I know that you said that if this ever happened I could still come to you with my problems, but I can't. It's not the same anymore.

I cried every day for the first 8 days. It's not that I can't live without you; it's that I don't want to even try. My roommates say that I deserve better, but I can't seem to believe them. I can put up with all your crap—I WANT to put up with all your crap—if it means being able to be with you. You have put up with all of mine; through the most of my depression. You have encouraged me, believed in me, cared about me, and loved me more than I ever thought was possible, and that's why I can't seem to let you go. My heart aches without you.

We have gotten to the point where we talk semi-regularly, but it's not the same. I just feel like I'm bothering you, like you aren't obligated to talk to me since we aren't dating anymore. We are going to dinner and a movie tomorrow, but is it a date? I don't know how to be just friends with you. I have become so dependent on you, and I almost hate myself for it. I know I can be stronger than this, but I've been strong for too long, and I crave to be weak. I crave to be wanted, to be needed, by someone. I don't want to be alone.

Please come back.

Love,
Me

▪▪

Patrick,
I know you're capable of loving someone. Sometimes I still wish it could've been me.
Andrea

Dear Dad,

Writing to you makes me feel like I'm 6 again. like I'm 6, and
you're not dead, and you don't hate me, and the world
consists of finger-painting and rainbows.
but dad, finger-painting leaves a mess, and rainbows only
come after rain.
I caught a dragonfly today. It reminded me of how when we
went to our old cottage, me and Brian would kneel in the
shallow water of the beach and stand as still as we could to
see if dragonflies would land on our outstretched palms.
He always caught more than me.
Dad, I miss you.
I hate you,
I love you,
and I miss you.
Do you have any idea how confusing that is?
Oh, and you remember Liam? well, we fell in love.
Obviously you were wrong by saying it was a little crush and
that he was no good and that what I wanted wasn't him
because what I wanted him to do wasn't what he would ever
do for me and that friendship bracelet was nothing more than
pipe-cleaners that stab you in the wrist with their sharp
edges.
You honestly haven't missed much — not that you would
notice if you were still here.
Basically,
you died.
Ryan died.
Liam and I made up.
Liam and I fell in love again.
Liam and I became the only thing I think about.
And you died, again.
Only this time, it was the essence of you that died — the
very existence of your memory.
(Considering I'm writing to you now, erasing you from my
memory didn't really work.)
And this year when your birthday comes, I'll attach this note
to the helium balloon, instead of items that are so heavy they
weigh the balloon down instead of floating upwards.

And this time,
maybe you'll read it.

(oh yeah, and: love Luc.)

Dear Grandfather,

I just want to start this off by saying that I'm glad you're dead. I find it amazingly hilarious and ironic that you were beaten to death by the other inmates – a fitting way to die for a man who beat his five year old granddaughter black and blue. You stole my innocence and wonder at the world.

Mom has always tried to convince me to write you a letter and forgive you, but I simply can't. It seems to me, that if I forgive you for sexually and physically abusing me for 7 years, then it makes it ok. But it's not. It never has been, and it never will be alright. Now that you're dead, I find that I can write you a letter and tell you how much you've scarred me. I couldn't give you the satisfaction of knowing you still haunted me while you were alive.

I struggled for many years after you were imprisoned, trying to deal with myself. I hated myself for letting you hurt me, for being unable to stop you. But I was five when it started, and you were 50. You had a gun, and as you told me, you weren't afraid to use it. What did it feel like, to press a gun into a small child's head and threaten to pull the trigger if she told anyone? Did it make you feel more like a man? I must admit though, you were a master manipulator. How did you manage to turn the fear of you into a hatred of myself? Even after you were far away from me, I still heard your voice in my head, whispering everything you had made me come to believe. "You are ugly. You are not worthy of love. Everyone hates you. You will never be good enough." Sadly enough, it seemed true, especially since my parents seemed too shell shocked and too busy with their own pain to even care that inside I was screaming. By then though, I was able to hide from everyone how much I was hurting, how hollow and empty life seemed. No one guessed. But you knew, didn't you? Did it make you laugh, when you were sitting there in your solitary cell, knowing that I was living in agony?

I lived in a deep, dark depression for five years after you were arrested. The Child Protective Services psychiatrists only wanted to push me for details in order to build the case against you, they didn't care about how I was afraid of the dark at thirteen, or how I woke up screaming every night, or how I hated everything about myself. Even then it was only about you. I started cutting myself hoping that I could leech you out of my blood, hoping that the more blood I spilled the less control you would have over me. It never worked, but I kept trying. I attempted to kill myself five different times, but every time I was never good enough at it and always woke up the next morning.

You know, you were the worst insult I've ever been given. My father thought that he could have me if you could. But I was older this time and smarter. I screamed and screamed and screamed until he stopped. He spit on me and told me "If I was your grandfather you'd let me." I haven't spoken to him since.

I crawled out of the depression and have started to live my life. I've learned to never let anyone walk on me or to believe the insults that might get thrown my way. They say that what doesn't kill you only makes you stronger, and it's true. I am a strong, passionate, driven woman now, and I smile when I think of you. Because, the joke is on you. You're the one who was attacked every time they let you out of solitary confinement. You're the one who never got any visitors or letters of endearment. Your family sided with me. If anyone ever goes to your grave, it will be to spit on it. No one you ever loved has loved you for ten years. Even the crooks hate you. They killed you for me, and I want to thank them.

And despite what you told me then, I now know that I am worthy of love. I've found a wonderfully kind, sensitive, generous man who comforts me when I wake up from a nightmare. He listens when I hesitatingly tell him of my past and doesn't push me. He loves me, despite all my flaws and has helped me to build my self confidence and self love. We're getting married in three months, and I am looking forward to the blessed years ahead with this man.
I know that what you did helped to shape the person I am now. I think I'm a pretty decent person, so in a strange way I should thank you. But I'm not going to, because you're still a bastard in my opinion.
With a lightened heart,

Me

Dear Steve,

Why did you have to do what you did? Why were you so STUPID to jump out in the street and get hit? You could have prevented that if you would have been patient. I was only 9. Do you really think it was fair for a 9-year-old girl to go through what I did? But still, I miss you. It has been what, 8 years now? And I have outlived you. You didn't even make it to graduation. You died before. I watched you waste away for 2 months. We all did. Hoping you would get better...I knew that you wouldn't. And to be honest, I am glad. Glad that you didn't have to live as a veggie. I always wonder how it would have been. If I hadn't lost one of 5 brothers. Would we have been close? Would I be a different person? Would I be skinny and popular? Would I not be a total outcast living outside the real world? I don't know. And I never will. It changed me for sure. And it changed our family. I hate myself for losing your memory. Not remembering your voice. Or how you looked besides one picture hanging on my wall. I still cry about you, you know. Sometimes I don't think of you. But other times I do. It hurts. Most people my age don't know what it feels like to lose someone. I do. Oh how I do. It sucks that we don't even mention much about you. We moved on it seems. I haven't. I will always miss you even though I barely knew you. I barely knew you. I never got the chance to grow up all the way with you. I will never forgive you for dying even though it wasn't your entire fault. But I just want you to know, even if time gets rid of everything I know about you, I will NEVER forget you. For as long as I live. Never. I hope you really are up there watching me. I hope you don't think I am that much of a total loser.
Love always from your little sister,
Janel Rose

∎∙∙∙∎

Dear Jim,

I'm sorry I fought with you the day you died. If I had known when you got into that car that you would be dead five minutes later, I would have hugged you and told you how much you meant to me. You meant the world to me. I never got to say goodbye. I will be living with that guilt for the rest of my life. It is the storm, the waves that I fight daily. I wonder if you really did love me. People say you did because you were my brother. Do you remember that fight that we had three days before the car accident? The one where I said that I wish you were dead? Dear God, I wish that fight never had happened. Brothers fight. I know this, but I wish we never had. My guilt is my hell…
Joe

∎∙∙∙∎

Dear God,
I just want to say thank you so much for turning my life around. It was so hard two years ago and even last year a bit, but now it's better than it's ever been, better than I ever could have imagined.
Even though lately there's been a few bumps along the road, I just can't believe how far I've come. From hating life being in a new city with no friends, to having so many people who I never want to lose and finally feeling happy. It's amazing, and so are you.
Love, Me

Dear Brandon,

Why is it that God "puts people in your life for a reason" and then rips them right back out? I knew the moment I met you that I loved you. It seems so ridiculous to say, but there was never any question in my mind. Apparently, there was no question in everyone else's mind either. Everyone knew.

I worked so hard to get that time alone with you, and it was the best time of my life. No one will ever hold me the way you held me. I will never feel that safe again. No one will ever kiss me the way you kissed me. I will never feel that spark again. No one will ever make love to me the way you did. I will never feel that wanted again.

You died. I thought there was no way to make it, but I did (only because of my little girl). We are coming up on the 1 year anniversary of your death. I am leaving home for the weekend. No one can see the amount of pain I'm still in. I want to go lay on your grave because that is the closest I can be to you. My heart died that day with you. As corny as it sounds, I will never find the feelings I had for you here on this earth.

We had our problems, but I loved you more than you will ever know. I will never be able to love like that again. Too much of me went with you in the accident. I pray that one day we can be together again. It's the only way I believe I will be happy.

With all my heart,
Broken

P.S. Please help take care of my Mom up there. I miss her. I know you will be there for her. She loved you too. I love you.

Dear God,

Hey. How are You? Good, I hope. Maybe You don't even have bad days. I would hope that it makes You happy when I turn off my radio in the car so I can talk to You. A lot has happened to me this past month. You know that. I know You're trying to show me what's going on and that I just don't get it yet.

I know You created him exactly how he should be. I also know You put him in my life for a reason. What I don't get is why You gave me such strong feelings for him, and him strong feelings for me, if he is meant to be gay. Why do we inspire each other so much? Why can't we ever be replaced in each others' hearts? Why do we understand each other like nobody else does, and why do I feel like the love I have for him is the kind of love You want all of us to experience?

I guess it's just proof that it's not all about sex. There's a lot of friendship that goes into a relationship. I just hope there is someone out there who has both aspects and who sees me for who I really am. Somebody who will love me unconditionally and want to spend his life with me.

Thanks for listening.
- A tiny bit of your creation

Dear Grandpa,

Why did you have to leave me when you did? You told me that night that you were feeling tired because of your bronchitis and that you would call me the next day because you had something you wanted to tell me.

When I was in Spanish class the next day, I saw your number on my caller-id. It seemed a little early but that was fine. When I called back, Grandma answered and all she did was say call your Mom. I called Mom at the office and her secretary said to call her cell phone. I did. She said you were gone. I wailed. I cried harder than I ever did in my life. My friend drove me home from class because I could hardly walk without falling over.

That was 2 and a half years ago.

Did you know I just graduated college? You said you would be there when I graduated. You said you wanted to see your oldest granddaughter graduate college. Why weren't you there watching me as I received my diploma? It took everything in my system to not cry as I walked across that stage because all I wanted was for you to be there with me.

Yesterday at my graduation party, cousin Sue said that she can just hear your voice saying how wonderful I looked and how proud you were. She said that I was your favorite and that you always sang my praises to the sky. Thank goodness another guest walked in to make sure I didn't break down in tears.

You, not Mom or Dad, raised me. You raised me to be the woman I am today. Because of you I go and get manicures and pedicures to occasionally treat myself. Because of you my daily Saturday morning routine is bank-dry cleaner-breakfast. Because of you, I listen to 20's music and sing "Me and My Shadow" when I need some inspiration. Because of you I know how to communicate properly with customers, clientele, family, and friends. Because of you, I know how to be passionate, strong, and courageous. Because of you, I am almost happy. If you were here I would be happy.

I just want your advice still -- need your advice still. I want to know what you think of this boy I'm in love with -- you were right when you said my last boyfriend wasn't right for me. Then again, you're always right. I want to know what you think of this new curriculum I'm designing and how I should change it. I want to know what you think I should do about our family feuding. I don't know how to fix the aunts fighting anymore. How did you do it?

I want to just sit in the car with you listening to our 20's music and singing "Me and My Shadow" once more. I just want to hear your voice again, see you again, spend one more day with you. If I ever get asked the question, who would you like to be caught in an elevator with, the answer is you.

I wish I knew what you wanted to tell me that Sunday night 2 1/2 years ago. Did you want to tell me a story about the past? Did you want to tell me something about the family? Did you want to give me advice on my degree? Did you want to make sure I didn't do something incredibly stupid? Did you just have a good joke to tell me?

There isn't a day I don't miss you. There isn't a day I don't think of you. There isn't a time when I don't wish I could have you around. If I can be half the person you are, I will be a successful woman in life.

I hope to see you again one day. I do hope there's a heaven where we can drive around singing "Me and My Shadow" again with no worries.

Your most beloved granddaughter,
Pooh bear

Dear Maranda,

It's so different around here now that you're gone. Some days it seems impossible to go on without you and the babies. The day you, Adam and Melina died I lost a part of myself. December 17, 2006 is a day the will be permanently etched in my heart. I miss seeing your smiling face every day, the way you walked into a room smiling seemed to make everyone else smile too. I remember the long nights we spent awake with Adam and Melina because they were difficult babies. It makes me sad to think about all the things we will never get to do or the things Adam and Melina will never get to do. When you died you left a four-year-old daughter behind. She is six now, and the family does everything they can to make sure she remembers you, Adam and Melina! I see so much of you in her, and it kills me that she won't get to know what a wonderful person you were. I have so many questions that are unanswered and will remain that way. I wish someone could explain why you and your babies were taken from us. Why you had to die at such a young age. But most of all I wish I knew what really happened that night. The pain of losing you and the babies will always be fresh, but I know you're in heaven smiling down with that beautiful smile of yours. You and the babies are truly missed and we love you all so much!!!
R.I.P
Maranda 23, Melina 1, and Adam Jr. 1
(December 17, 2006)

Dear Lost Love,

It has been almost a year since that day. I will never forget when Dad walked through the door and told me you were gone. You had been killed in a car accident, and he wouldn't let anyone else tell me. I wanted to beat on him and call him a liar, but all I could do was run. I went through the next days in a haze until we went to the viewing, and I actually saw you, it was easier to be in denial without seeing you. The next morning, at the church, I was able to touch you and tell you good-bye, and my world stopped in that moment. I have been walking through life with no idea where I am headed. All I know is I want it to lead to you. I miss you more every day. I tried to "move on," and that was a horrible disaster. There will never be another you; there will never be anyone to make me feel that way again.

I love you,
Shattered

••

Dear God,

Thanks for restoring my faith. And my happiness for that matter. I know that this happens a lot. That life gets hard but then sooner or later things work out in the end. I know it's because of You, and I know that I shouldn't lose my faith every time, but it's just hard sometimes. So thank You for for never giving up on me.
I've never been happier :D

Dear God,

I'm sure this wasn't your goal, your purpose for creation. I know Adam and Eve messed up big time, but you loved them anyway. Cain killed Abel, but you still loved him, you marked him but did not destroy him. Humans are not perfect, not by a long shot, but you already know that. Hell, you made us this way.

Not that I am blaming you or anything, quite the contrary, I just have so many unanswered questions that no one seems to agree upon. So many different denominations and religions, with so many different rules, God is God after all; whether it's Yahweh or Allah, it is still the same thing. What's in a name anyway? Just letters strung together, nothing more. What if the name I have wouldn't have been the name you chose for me, what if Emily was really supposed to be Hannah or Leah (sorry God I digress, the Jon and Kate marathon is on, but still you know what I mean).

It's so hard deciding for myself what you think or want me to do and be. I don't believe you want me to be unhappy; you don't want me to suffer like before. Nine years of depression and finally I am pulling myself out, aren't you proud?? I hope you are, I know in my heart you love me, so what's the big deal. I am not going to get pregnant and get an abortion, I am not going to marry some deadbeat and get a divorce. I am going to live with my girlfriend and be happy. I am going to live, and continue to live. The years of waiting for death are over; the years of happiness and joy are upon me.

They tell me you are not happy, they tell me I am living in sin, and I will suffer for it. Suffer?! Seriously?! I suffered for years without it, without this feeling of love and belonging, last time I checked suicide was also a sin. I guess I just chose the lesser of two evils, but I don't truly believe that, and I don't think you do either. You made me. And I am grateful that you made me what I am, I just wish I had figured it all out sooner, the years of wasting away and wasting my life were an insult to you and your goodness. But I have changed and I will continue to do so, for the better, against all odds.

Thanks for your time.
Talk to you later.
In the name of the Father, the Son, and the Holy Spirit. Amen.

Love, Em

Dear Cat,

Thank you for being here for me all the time. I guess you didn't really have a choice after I scooped you up out of that ice storm.

You always know exactly what I need. A head lick to make me laugh, a belly kneading when I'm feeling bad, face kisses when I'm feeling lonely, a frisky pounce when I'm feeling playful. You're perfect. You make me want to be a crazy cat lady someday, with 20 cats just like you.

I wish I could've known you as a kitty. I think we would've gotten along even back then. You've picked up and can perfectly mimic my moods after a short year and a half, I can only imagine how close we'd have been if we grew up together.

Sorry I call you fatty. It's just because you've more than doubled your weight, from 6 to 15 pounds, since I've known you. But I really do love how your belly pools around you when you're lounging. And the way that you look like a penguin when you sit because I can't see your feet.

I'm glad you found and adopted me.

Mom

Dear Scars,

I am terribly in love with you. It's weird but whenever you start to fade I want to add more. You're my battle wounds, and I need you to feel alive.
I need you to remind me that I am human – that I can and should feel it all. The pain is a drug to me, and you are the receipt, the proof of the transaction between me and the blade.
And you're beautiful. You change the pigment of my skin from pink to brown, I look down and see you, and you are gorgeous to me, yet hideous to the world.
My mother fears you, simply because she refuses to see you for what you really are. You're an accident to her, nothing more. And although she did not cause you to appear, she should take the blame for not noticing the pain that resulted in your creation.
You were an addiction for so long, an addiction I have tried to wean myself off of but like any other addiction it is an ongoing struggle. And I can always fall off the wagon. And I have. Sadly my wrists have become too noticeable, and I have to find alternative places to add you to my collection. You are my body art, and just like a tattoo, the relief I feel from you is a breath of fresh air in the harsh reality of the world.
People don't understand addicts like me, I don't want to die. And you know that. I simply want to feel, and most of the time I don't. I can't feel you when blood runs out of the shallow and deep cuts alike, I know I should, but I don't. That's why we continue to cut, so that one day we can feel that pain, and it will be better.

Today I don't need you, and although I want to say it with confidence that I do not need you anymore, I can't get rid of you just yet and part of me never wants to. I love you too much.
So thanks for always being there for me.
Danke, ich liebe dich.

Love, me

Dear Anger,

Why do you come so easily? I don't even have to be really paying attention to what someone is saying or doing for me to be angry. It's like your lurking in the dark depths of my sub-conscience waiting not so patiently to tap into my conscience mind and interfere with my everyday life. You don't moderate; you seem to come full force each time you appear. You've hurt people and done reckless things. I wish I had more control over you; I will conquer you one day. I will no longer stand for this.

Your Victim,
Hurt and Never Painless

Dear Pot,

It has been many years since we first met. I was but a young girl, and you were mysterious and seductive. We have been nearly inseparable since. Yes we have had our up and downs, but what relationship hasn't. I would like to take this chance to highlight the finer points and lower points of our journey through life together.

I remember when we were new in our relationship, I would get so hyper every time you were around, You would appear, and I would talk for hours, about everything and anything. I remember when I told the entire room that there was a tribe of little people living in my mouth and every time I talked they jumped on my tongue to make my words come out of my mouth. I was giddy and excited constantly near you. You made me insanely happy, and we were monogamous for about a year or two.

You were my muse for many creative writing assignments. Remember that paper about the lady and the tiger? The one where the whole class was crying because they were laughing so hard? If it weren't for you, I could have never come up with that.

You have also helped my passion for the culinary arts. No one but you could have inspired such creations such as dill pickles dipped in salsa and ranch. And cookie dough rolled up inside of bologna. That is efficiency if I have ever heard of it.

Remember that one time that after spending quality time with you, I couldn't stop talking in a southern accent for hours?! Looking back, I wonder why more people didn't catch on to us.

I wish it could have been just me and you forever, but some of the people you hung with began to look attractive, and as you are aware, I haven't always been faithful to just you. I know you know this because you have been present more often than not. I am sorry I broke up with you temporarily to date your shady cousin, coke. I knew he was no good for me, but sometimes a girl has got to be bad. Your friends and I have always flirted, but no one will ever replace you.

I remember when my mother discovered our love. You weren't there that day. I am glad. God only knows what she would have done to you. She told me I was forbidden to ever love you again, to ever touch you again, to ever even see you again. I played coy, yes. I even took a small break from you, but much like Romeo and Juliet, our love was too deep for parental disapproval to separate us for good.

We spent every day together my junior year in high school. I was with you before, after and during school. I even saw you once in my classroom under a desk. You sneaky, sneaky little thing.

We got used to each other, and our relationship became much more relaxed. It was pretty common for us just to hang out with some other friends and watch a movie or listen to some Pink Floyd.

Now we have been together for the better part of nine and a half years. And we are as close as ever, I have seen you 3-4 times a week for the last year or so. In fact, seeing you about an hour ago inspired me to write this letter.

Do I have any regrets? No, I absolutely do not. You have been the love of my life. My life would be much less exciting without you. And although my mother still despises you, you have never had a problem with being a secret love. And I appreciate you for that.

Unfortunately, I foresee an indefinitely long break in the near future for us. I am trying to put off this parting as long as physically possible because I love you. I never want to live without you, but there are those who say we can't be together. People who may offer me employment and a secure future. Things you have never been able to offer me. I know this sounds shallow and materialistic, but I must go with them. You know you will always be in my heart, and hopefully we can meet on the sly after I have secured such a job.

I love you and thank you for all the great times,
Sunshine

P.S. Thank you for helping me understand tie-dye and Radiohead music videos.

Dear Heart,

Why do you always get me into trouble? Why do you never agree with my head? Why do you make my decisions so difficult? I guess you're down there, inside of me, trying to be heard, trying to look out for me. I'm sorry my brain shoots you down so often. I'm sorry that both logic and the society I grew up in tell me to ignore you. I'm sorry I confuse you with lust and infatuation. Show me how to really feel you and follow you. Show me how to be true to you, and use your messages instead of being mistrustful of them. Speak to me a little louder. Beat a little faster when I get something right for once. Make me realize it when you're speaking to me. Tell me what I need to hear. Be illogical, but appeal to logic enough that you two can work together to bring me to a conclusion. Ich weiss nicht was ich will. Aber du weisst es. Mache es klar, bitte. Help me love people as much as I possibly can. Help me stay happy throughout the day. Inspire me a little bit. Don't leave me high and dry.
Don't ever let me look back at the past few months and think, "Oh wow, where did that go, and what of importance did I do?" Come alive inside of me, please. Be stronger than my head. Please.

With love,
LB

••

Dear Homework,
Go to Hell.
You ruin my life, every single day. Why must you have to occupy my life for countless hours every night and leave me stressed out, usually in tears?
The feeling sucks and so do you.
So just go away.
Okay, thanks.

••

Dear Timing,

You suck. I hate you. You always rip me from the people I love. I know you're trying to teach me a lesson, but you always take so long to reveal to me what I need to learn!

Begrudgingly,
LB

••

Dear Depression,

I feel alone.

Dear Puppy,
I know you are hungry, but no one gets rudely woken up at 5 a.m. and is happy about it. Please take this into consideration tomorrow morning.

Promising treats if you comply,
Your Owner

Dear Guy-Who-Deserved-Better,
I broke up with you in the parking lot just after a performance. No proper "goodbye," no time to talk anything out, only "this is getting really awkward, can we stop this whole dating thing and just be friends?" I still remember the look on your face-- so confused and clearly hurt. I don't even remember what you said, only that I was in such a selfish hurry to do the deed that I ran to my friend's car as soon as the conversation was ended, jumped in and told her to drive away as fast as possible. At the time I only remember feeling relieved. At last, weeks of awkwardness put to an end with one swift blow! But now I see how selfish my actions were. You were so kind to me. You made me laugh, and we could talk about anything for any length of time. You were (and still are, I trust) always considerate and trustworthy. I never even fully expressed to you why I broke it off. At the time it just seemed easier to brush you aside as quickly as possible with as little explanation as possible so that I could avoid any unpleasantness.

Thing is, I might have gotten off with minimal discomfort, but I know I hurt you deeply. In my selfish haste, I caused you great pain and for that I am truly sorry. I don't regret breaking up with you-- it was high school, and what the heck did we know about love?? But I am sorry for how I did it. You deserved so much better. Ironically, I really did want to still be your friend, but my selfishness cost me your friendship. My just deserts, I suppose. Thankfully I have learned how to respect those I love. Too bad I didn't know better at the time. I'm sure none of this would even interest you today, but after five years of holding it in, I just had to say

I'm sorry.

~J

Paul,

You are so unbelievably attractive. I can't stop thinking about how sexy you are. The moment we met I knew there was something between us. This is problematic seeing as I have a boyfriend... Ugh, I feel so guilty when we spend time together, not only because they feel like dates (and I do miss that date-y feeling) but also because I intentionally refuse to ever bring my boyfriend up in conversations, even though I know you and me are just friends.

Sometimes I think that if you ever were to make a move that I'd be okay with that... that I'd leave my boyfriend and fall in love with you. Sometimes I secretly wish we could just have one hot night and never tell my boyfriend. I do know, however, that he would leave me in two seconds if I ever messed around with any other guy... and I know that's legit but that might be all I need to get over it and recommit. Then again, my boyfriend is great, and I would feel awful keeping that secret or even leaving him if I didn't know he'd find someone else to love and be happy with.

I'm hoping this is just a phase, so for now I'm going to just pray that you won't present me with that you-or-he ultimatum, as I'm not quite ready to make that choice yet.

Me

∎ •

Dear potential love interest,

I know it's not unique or special to have a crush. But every time it happens to me, it feels like it is. You fell out of the sky one day when I wasn't looking for it and didn't expect it. Now, even though in reality nothing has changed, all my days seem to sparkle with the possibility of you. Bob Dylan said he knew he had feelings for a girl when she brought out the poet in him, and I guess I feel the same way, even though I'm no Bob Dylan. But you've become a muse for me, and that doesn't happen very often, which is how I know I think of you as more than a random body in space.

I can't even explain what it is about you that infatuate me. I guess "adorable" is the best adjective to describe your appearance, but it's something more than that. Your presence is a breath of fresh air, and I know that's clichéd but it's also true. You have an indefinable way of conducting yourself that insists on goodness and truth and wholesomeness and honor, and the way your eyes crinkle when you smile doesn't hurt, either.

My favorite part is that we've only just met, so I have plenty of time to gather up all the delicious charms and quirks of your personality and add them to my portrait of you on the canvas in my head. As you become more whole, I will fall harder for you, or not. Maybe you will fade away, and all I will have is this brief moment of potential to remember fondly. If you continue to grow brighter, though, I hope I will be able to declare my affection for you in bold and unequivocal terms. It's too early to think about any future other than tomorrow, but I'm nothing if not patient. I can only hope that whatever comes out of this will be worth the wait.

Love, maybe,
Another random body

Dear Mom,

This is not going to be long, but I just wanted to thank you for everything you have done for me my whole life. I know I was a bit of a handful in high school and not quite what you expected of me, and I know I still can give you quite a bit of grief, but I also know you are very proud of me and what I have accomplished since then. Thank you for never losing faith in me and for always supporting me through thick and thin (especially financially). You and Dad have both always been there for me and always support my educational endeavors no matter what the cost, and it means a lot. I promise there will be a large turn around for you, and you'll be able to live a long, happy life and not have to worry about finances after too long ever again. Thanks for being a great mother.

Banana

Dear Dad,

I don't know why, but all I can do is tell you I hate you. You and everyone else know that. Or at least that's what you think. I really do love you. I used to miss you so much. But I got tired of that. Now, all I miss is the Dad that you could have been, used to be.

You say that you were there for me, that you never left. Maybe not physically, but all you knew was that you were in la la land getting high off of some Percocet and Valium. That's all you ever cared about, your drugs.

Mom says you didn't know what you were doing; it was the doctor prescribing all of this. You just did what you were told. But you knew. At one point, you just know when you have no emotion other than anger and all you do is abuse your three children. You were always strict with my brothers. But your little girl? The little girl you never thought you would have. The little girl that you would have done anything for? You abandoned her.

You were my dad for crying out loud! You were supposed to be there for me. We were supposed to be a family. I didn't choose this. I didn't ask for an addictive father. It wasn't in my plans. But it was chosen for me. Every time that you hit me and every time that you grabbed me. I begged you to stop. But you never did. You didn't even know how bad you were. Because you just forgot it the next day.

I honestly don't know how you live with yourself. After all of the hell and crap you put me through. After everything you said to me. After you treated me like crap and trash and abused me, how do you come home every day and look at me and not feel guilt and self inflicted pain because you put your precious little girl in harm's way. The one you would do anything for, remember? Yeah, a load of bull that was. All Mom ever does is make excuses for you. Well you can't excuse that. And you can't redo 13 years. The damage is done, and I'm the one who has to take the toll for your mistakes.

Mom told me we were getting out. I honestly wish she knew how to keep her word. I can't look at you without thinking of how much better our relationship would be. After all of the things you did to her? How does she deal with you?

I want you to know that I don't hate you. But I don't love you either. Because you never loved me. All I can do is miss you. And imagine. But I don't want a relationship. I've seen you at your worst. And after that, your best isn't something I want to see.

I don't wish to change this. You chose this. And I'm not open for you to come in.

Your daughter,
Jessica

Dear Mom,

Why do you ALWAYS have to deprive me of my teenage years? It's not like I'm going to stay in high school forever or live here with you forever. I know that I'm your "baby" but still. I NEED to leave the house. As for Rose, I know she's a little handicapped but I mean, GIVE me a BREAK! It's not like she's TOTALLY helpless. She can stay home by herself for a couple hours. That's the longest I'm EVER gone. So I don't know why you have to come up with excuses like, "What if a tornado was to come up? She'd be home all by herself." MOM. It's fall. Almost winter. I'm PRETTY sure there aren't going to be any tornadoes.

As for the trust? What the CRAP is up with that?! I have NEVER done anything bad or "bad". If you're thinking of the lying, then it's your own fault. Because I wouldn't have to lie if I knew you wouldn't get mad or ground me or whatever. My friends have and probably will continue to drink. But I just want you to know: I've NEVER drank! I've had chances. Not only that but to smoke! And to have sex too. But I haven't done ANY of those things. I cuss once in a while but it's normal. Even YOU do it! So don't give ME that bull crap! Cause I don't want to hear it! I'm not perfect, and I know it. Not going to church? That day I really did feel sick. And you didn't believe me! It's not like YOU WANT to go to church EVERY Sunday. So don't give me that. I DREAD going to church. For multiple reasons. I know everyone always tells me, "Those are the best people to be with. They share the same morals as you, and they're good people." You and I both know that's not entirely true. People leave the Church all the time because people are jerks. And people have been jerks to me and also they are rude and talked behind my back. You've had it happen to you.

Getting mad at me for going on walks or jogs with friends? Big deal. I don't know why you can't just let me do it. It's healthy, and I want to do it, so back off. It's not like I tell you I'm going for a walk or a jog and sneak away to have sex. I don't do that!

My trip to Europe. It's probably going to be a once in a life time thing, and my friends are going and it's not like it's just teenagers, so I'll be "safe".

I NEED a new car more than I want it. And you know this. Who cares what the older kids think, or about the insurance going up. Quit wasting your money on stupid stuff. I understand you wanting to buy something for yourself once in a while... It's understandable.

If I don't want to come home at all right when you call, I shouldn't have to. You should trust me enough to come home when I'm ready. Or if I want to spend the night at a girl's house it's NOT a big deal. I WON'T have sex! One of them is a lesbian, but I still love her to death. The other has a boyfriend, and her mom would kill me. The others would put us in a different room AND different floor. And they would like-wise kill me. I wouldn't want to have sex anyways. My luck they would get pregnant. Because we have such bad luck. It's gross.

I may thank you when I'm older... but I doubt it. Most of the time I only love you because I have to. You're such a jerk sometimes, and I'm pretty sure you gave the older kids more freedom than me. But it's probably only because all my friends are girls but whatever. But it's not like that should matter. If you trust me like you SAY you do, then don't make a big deal. One of your other concerns is what if people hear about it? People spend the night at other people's houses all the time. Guys and girls. Girls and guys. Like that one time I went away for the weekend? And I said I was in another room than the girls? Yeah. Well we all slept in the same room. A gay guy and THREE other girls! And guess what?! We didn't do ANYthing! But of course I didn't tell you that. Why? Because you would FLIP. And you know it so I can't always tell you the truth or the whole truth even if we didn't do anything. But OK. Whatever.

-Your Son

Dear Dad,

People have told me for a long time how remarkable it is that we've all come through the divorce without getting angry or bitter. They all say how strong we are for being able to maintain good relationships all around. It's been ten years, and while they mean well, I just wish they wouldn't say things like that to me anymore. I don't feel remarkable or strong or wonderful. I feel hurt.

I'm glad you and Mom were able to maintain a cordial relationship. It saved us a lot of grief and trauma as kids. I thank you for being a wonderful father, supportive and involved and caring. You've always given more than was asked of you, and you've never murmured a word of complaint or resentment. I feel so humbled and grateful that out of all the divorce scenarios, we got almost the best one. I just wish it didn't have to happen. I'm an adult now, and a part of me still feels like that shocked and heartbroken little girl who found out her family was being rent asunder. Since those dark days, I've found out a lot of things about the situation. I know what happened, and I know it's your fault. We've spoken about it, but you don't like to because you know in your heart that it was your doing. This isn't Mom poisoning me against you - she's always been respectful of you. I learned what happened, I know about the affair. I blame you for everything.

I love you so much, and I am not really angry with you, but in my secret heart I am hurt and confused. The way you live your life now... the things you've done in the past... the way you betrayed Mom... I just don't know how to process it. Mom isn't perfect, and she can be really annoying sometimes, but nobody IS perfect, Dad. If men are only faithful to perfect women, then what does that mean for me - a very imperfect girl? I see the women you've dated, and I've watched the way you've played them because you can't decide who you like better. You are a coward, and you cheat on women. What am I supposed to think about men when the man I've loved most in this world acts like that?

My biggest point, Dad, is that because of you and your life I find myself unable to trust men in a relationship setting and for that matter any living person in a friend setting. The man of my dreams has come along, and he wants to offer me the most beautiful life with him, but because of you I find myself too scared to accept. You were, and still largely are, a good man and you both were very in love when you married Mom. Somewhere along the way, you lost that love and sought it somewhere else. How do I know that won't happen to me? I don't know how to have a successful marriage because you didn't show me. I don't know how to take that leap of faith; I don't know how to trust that in 10 years he'll still love me like he does now.

I wish you could see how much more you messed up than just a marriage.
I still love you. I always have. You've caused me more tears than anyone else in the world, but they've all been because I care so much about you. Just please tell me something that will make all this confusion and pain disappear. Promise it won't happen to me too.
Love,
Your Little Girl

Dad,

Back in 2000, you were simply my mom's boyfriend. You were a stranger in my house, and I did my best to make you feel unwelcome. Not talking to you; trying to undermine you; anything I could do to try to get you out. But you never budged. You stuck around. I thought it was because you loved my mother, but I began to see there was more to that story. You actually loved us; my mom, my brother and me. You took us in as if we were your own. You helped me in any chance you could. You woke up at 4 o'clock on Wednesdays, which were your day off, to teach me how to drive a stick. All through high school, you raised me as your own, even though we had no blood connection. Even though you and my brother had MANY fights, you still treated him as if he was your own son, even though he didn't reciprocate that feeling. You've helped him since day one: rather it was with his "situation" or anything else. And you continue, until this day, to help me in any way possible. Nine years with you have made us a family, and I am extremely blessed to have you in my life. I've heard so many horror stories about step-parents, but I'm so glad you weren't one of them.

Love,
Your son
Maurice

Mama Bear,

Thank you. Thank you for being a wonderful mother. Thank you for sending us to catholic school to get the best education. I am sorry for all the times I told you I hated you after daddy's death. I am sorry I gave you such a hard time until my senior year in high school. I am sorry it took me so long to grow up. Thank you for allowing me to go to a private university, I promise I will make you proud.

I am so proud to have you as my mother.

Love,
Your Youngest

To whoever,
I just need to get this out.
Sometimes, I feel like I hate my dad. Like, my life would be better if he just dropped dead or wasn't around. And it makes me sad, but it's true. Not all the time, but sometimes. It's hard to explain.
Sometimes he's so nice and awesome, and I know that he loves me and is proud of me. But the things that sometimes come out of his mouth are unbelievable to say the least. Things that I would never wish upon anyone to have said at them.
And the worst part is, whenever he says or does bad stuff, he acts like nothing happened, like he's the greatest father in the world. Like, why I never want anything to do with him is just because I'm a moody teenager who doesn't care about their parents.

Well, it's so much more than that.
And I kind of wish you could see that.
That what you do absolutely sickens me...The things you say to me, or to anyone else.
I've had enough.

Dear Mom,

You took so much from me with your alcoholism. I can't remember a night when I was able to go to sleep in peace. I was a child! How could you do that to me and still say that you love me?

I remember those nights, when I would wake to the sounds of you stumbling down the hallway. I faked being asleep when you would open my bedroom door and tell whichever drunk you would bring home that I was your "baby girl". I wonder if you remember that? I can't seem to forget it.
Do you regret your past? Even if you don't, I regret it for you.

Your Daughter.

Dear Mom,

I know we don't really do emotional things like have a good cry every now and then or tell each other about really personal feelings, and we especially don't dwell on the I-love-yous. However, just because I treat you more like a friend than a parent doesn't mean I don't appreciate all of the amazing things about you. I want you to know that every time you give me a hug and I shrug it off and every time you tell me you love me and get a mumbled response back, in my head I'm doing the opposite. I don't get to see you much anymore, and it's moments like these that make me homesick and sad that the wonderful childhood I had is over. So that's how I deal—I just don't do emotions.

You have always been the coolest mom in any circle of friends I've ever had. They love to be around you, and it makes me so proud that I can say, "Yeah, that's my Mom. Isn't she great?"

You've always trusted me and never tried to crush any of my ideas. When I ask for help, you're there to give it, and you always do it in a way that's all your own. You're such a smart woman, and I love it when people try to go one up on you because they can't. I hope I grow up to be like that.

You work so hard for your family, and we all appreciate it, even when we don't show it the way we probably should. Thanks for always making me feel good about myself—you're terrific.

Love,
Me

Mom,

I always seem to make mistakes whenever I do things for you. And I used to think that this was because I was never good enough, that I was the problem. But now I know that it's you. It's always been you.

Every single time I try and do something for you, you shut me down, and I feel useless and ashamed.

Other people say that they're proud of me and that they love me or that they think I have the potential to do anything I want to do, but I don't remember the last time I've heard you say any of those things.

I just feel like I'm a disappointment to you, and I just want to know why.

I want to be a teacher more than anything. It's my dream. You're a teacher, but you don't want me to be one because there aren't many jobs. So for support I talk to my teacher. At least she believes in me. And you know what the sad thing is? I'd rather spend time with my teacher than with my own mother. But I guess that's the way it is sometimes.

Even just little things I try to do to help you I always seem to make a mistake. How come you're never pleased? My room is never clean enough, my marks are never quite high enough, and my piano isn't quite perfect enough?

Don't you think it's strange how everyone else seems fine with how I'm turning out, except you? How, maybe, just once, one word of encouragement would be appreciated?

No? Didn't think so...

Well, there's always tomorrow.

Love, your daughter.

Dear Mom,

They tell me I have your eyes, your laugh, your hair and your smile. At times I wonder what parts of me are actually me and not you. When I was in high school Dad told me something that I will never forget. It haunts me almost daily because of the guilt and shame I feel. He said that sometimes he can't even look at me without wanting to cry because it hurt him too much to see you in me. How is anyone supposed to take something so lightly? I often find your sisters staring at me, and I can't help but wonder if it's hard for them to see me too, like I'm a constant reminder of such a horrible time in all our lives. Living my life was like growing up in the shadow of an older sibling except it was my own mother whose life I had to live up to. For so long I didn't want to be you, I wanted to be me. For once I wanted someone to recognize me for me and not automatically identify me with you. I never got the chance to be my own person. When I got my senior pictures taken in high school, it looked exactly like yours from when you were my age; I was horrified. A little over a year ago I came to terms with your death and my life as an extension of yours. I got a tattoo in honor of you, and it says "in me she lives," because after nearly 21 years of hating to be reminded of how much I was you, I realized it was a blessing instead of a curse. You are part of me, but I am not you, I am me. Around the same time I got my tattoo I started dating someone that I never thought would lead to anything. A year later I'm happy to say we're headed in a serious direction, but something he said to me recently made me wonder about you. He said sometimes when he looks at me I look like an angel. Part of me hopes that angel in me is actually you shinning through.
Your daughter,
MB

Dear Daddy,

Words are not enough to express how much you mean to me. Even while thinking about what I want to write to you I am having trouble because I don't really see a way that I can express my gratitude to you.

I think that ever since the day I was born I was your little girl. Mom always tells the story about how you wanted a boy and then when you found out my sex how you weren't even disappointed because you knew I would be better than any son ever could be. I know you would never admit it to my sister, but I think that I was always your favorite. We have everything in common, including our looks, and I could talk to you for hours about anything. You have told me you are worried about me finding some boy who is going to take your place, but I want you to know there will never be a better man in my life.

I know I don't always listen to you at times, and I know that it hurts you. I wish I could take all those terrible decisions back that caused you and Mom any kind of hurt. I am mostly sorry about Steven. I wish I would have told you earlier because waking up in the hospital and seeing you with that look in your eyes, a look mixed with hurt and anger and about 100 other emotions, was probably the most painful moment of my life. It hurt me more than my broken hand at the time. I am so sorry and so grateful. You truly were my guardian angel and still are, thank you, thank you, thank you for then and for everything.

I love you so much and cannot imagine having a better, more fun, more concerned and more amazing dad than you. You truly are my best friend. I love you.

Daughter

Dear Dad,
Thank you for emotionally scaring me permanently. I blame you.
-Your youngest and best.

Dear Mom,
We will never be as close as you want us to be. I'm sorry.
I love you to pieces,
Rachie

Dear Ex-Lifeguard,

You made this summer job so much fun for me. I always looked forward to walking down into the park at night with you, or driving down in one of the crappy park vehicles to return my bag of money after being on the cash register all day. I like that we both enjoyed the Ferris Wheel all lit up with lightning pulsing through the clouds behind it.

You're six or seven years older than me, and you've lived probably a very different life than I have, with some similarities (the Catholic school thing). But I'm honored that you would share some of your life experiences with a mere clerk. I'm glad you find me a trustworthy person to talk to. I wonder though, why you never asked me about myself? Maybe because you had to keep your professional manner with me. You are, after all, my boss. And of course, you get to weave the picture of yourself that you want me to have when you're the only one talking.

I take great pride in asking you a few questions that really made you think, though. And I'm sincerely interested in your well-being. That's just how I am. I like to challenge people to rethink why they do things. I don't want you to be lonely, if you don't really want to be. But if that theme park is what really fills your needs and gives you enough friendships to get by, then who am I to say otherwise? You are an adult, and you get to spend your life how you want to.

I'm a 19-year-old kid, I guess. I pretend I'm older because I want to be seen as someone worth listening to. I want people to know that I have a bit of wisdom in this cranium of mine. I love feeling like I'm a good addition to any group, that people trust me to do my job. Thanks for telling me I'm awesome. I think you're pretty awesome too, even if people up at the park take you for granted. You work your ass off and you actually care about how people are treated. That last one is a valuable trait, though I think lots of people at work overlook it.

You're going to make an excellent HR director someday, wherever you end up in the long run. Good luck with your studies, and don't underestimate your effect on people. You left a mark on me, even though I won't tell you so, because that would break our professional relationship. And I'd never do that to you. Your image is deep-rooted, and I'd never take it from you, or risk humiliating myself. But if someday your eyes run past this, know that you're a good person, and that I appreciate it.

Just don't ever mention this to me. We'll keep it a secret, okay? Then no one has to be made fun of for anything.

God Bless,
Whiteboard Artist

You say you want to know more about me, well here you go. Maybe this will give you some answers as to why I am the way I am.

I moved a lot as a kid. But I didn't mind. Then for four years I stayed in the same place...4th to 8th grade. I was one of the "popular kids," but I was nice to everybody in class. I was on every sports team, and pretty much every club. Yes, I was that person.

But then after 8th grade I moved again, really far away. New city, high school, I knew no one. I met some close friends, but I was suddenly the quietest person in all my classes. I wasn't involved in many school things, and I kept to myself mostly. Anyone from my old school probably wouldn't recognize me.

Then, on March 24th, God I hate March 24th...one of my best friends from my old school died. She killed herself. And I couldn't believe it. I still don't believe it. I just felt completely empty inside, I didn't know what to do, why it happened. Her name was Kayla. I hated her at first, and I feel terrible for things that I did, but then we became fairly close.

Then, on March 26th, God I hate March 26th...my grandpa died suddenly. A heart attack. No one saw it coming.

I guess you could say I was a disaster on the inside. But I didn't tell anyone. I mean, my family knew about my grandpa obviously, and my friends in my old city about my friend, but at my school nobody knew.

But I constantly thought about it. Like, if I never moved if things would have been different. I don't know. And I guess I never will.

Then after 9th grade I moved again. I got to my new school and knew absolutely no one. I had no friends, and I was broken on the inside. But I acted like everything was fine. I went to the library every single day at lunch because I didn't have any friends. And nobody wanted any new friends. That year was hell. Absolute hell. I was even quieter. Everyone asks why I am so quiet, and I say I don't know, but do you want to know why? It's because I think I don't deserve to talk. I know that that's a terrible thing to think, but it's true, I still think it today a lot. I just can't help it.

I still felt empty inside. I couldn't and still can't shake the death of my friend and my grandfather. I just think about that and everything else in my life, and I just don't feel anything.

I don't feel happy, because I feel like I don't deserve it, kind of like I don't deserve to talk. Like, I have no right to be happy because of things that I've done, because I've been here the shortest, because I'm less important.

But then last year something changed. You came along. You, my teacher. You were one of the nicest and funniest people I had ever met. So I took your class, loved your class and helped out in a class of yours the next semester. We became so close, and we still are. You are the only person who ever makes me feel happy.

You make me feel worthy. Like I can actually make something of my life. You inspire me, and you believe in me.

To tell you the truth, I do not know if I would still be here if it weren't for you. You're saving me. Every day.

You're saving me, and you don't even know it. Even though I've had a little bit of a tough beginning, I know that as long as I have you in my life, everything's going to be okay.

So you can't leave, okay?

Thanks,

Friends Forever xoxo

Dear high school biology teacher,

Here is my letter...story perhaps...It is an apology letter to a high school biology teacher named Mr. Schell....this incident has bothered me ever since, and sometimes I think I will find him in person and tell him my sorrowfulness....but I'm scared to.

I was new at this High school, but I knew many of the kids there. I was still trying to fit in. I think I was a second-semester freshman...

Biology was always a bore for me...and I wouldn't pay attention...I would daydream. The teacher, Mr. Schell, was kind of...well....I hate to say it now, but not the best looking man in the world...he would be what one would call a "geek."....BUT, he was VERY nice, and his wife was a teacher too....I didn't dislike him at all...just was bored in his class.

I had a best friend, Mary, whom I used to write letters to in school when I was bored and she did the same...So, here I was in Biology not concentrating and bored stiff...I decided to write Mary a letter...

I chose to write about the "geekiness" of Mr. Schell....it was bad. I listed about the most horrible physical qualities a guy could have...you see, Mary and I would basically have contests on who could be the most vulgar! We had fun, but it was generally innocent...this time it wasn't.

Like I said, I really liked Mr. Schell....so I think you will understand how sorrowful I was after the result of writing this letter during class....AND the subject matter....just think of the worst things someone could say about your face, your body...even your voice. I was awful.

Mr. Schell walked down the aisle, smiled at me and took the letter from my hands. I then had the most God-AWFUL feeling come and reside in my soul...when I think about it now that feeling comes back....it haunts me...

The next day in class, Mr. Schell walked up to me and handed the letter back to me! No words,,,again,,,just that smile....it was a kind smile...I cannot remember if I even said I was sorry because I just felt so badly!

So...this is my letter of apology to a teacher who had a heart of gold...and didn't deserve that kind of treatment from a student...

I feel a little better after writing this...but it doesn't matter how I feel now does it?

Carole P.

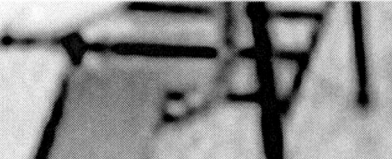

Dear Mrs. R,
You were my middle school choir teacher. You always told me I could do anything I put my mind to. You pushed me further than anyone I can remember and knew I deserved more than what I had. If the judges scored my solo lower than you thought, you made sure to tell me and you always had faith in me. Choir was what I looked forward to and what I mainly remember about middle school. You helped me so much, and it's sad to say that you will never know this. You changed schools, and I have no idea where you are now. I don't think I would be as much into singing and music and even acting were it not for you and your encouragement to keep going. You helped me into an advanced choir in high school, and I genuinely felt sad when I left 8th grade. I really wish I could see you now and tell you how much you meant to me. You helped so much during those awkward teenage years, and I hope you know how much of an effect you had on your kids. We all loved you. You helped us grow. I'll never forget you.
Sincerely,
Second soprano in the second row

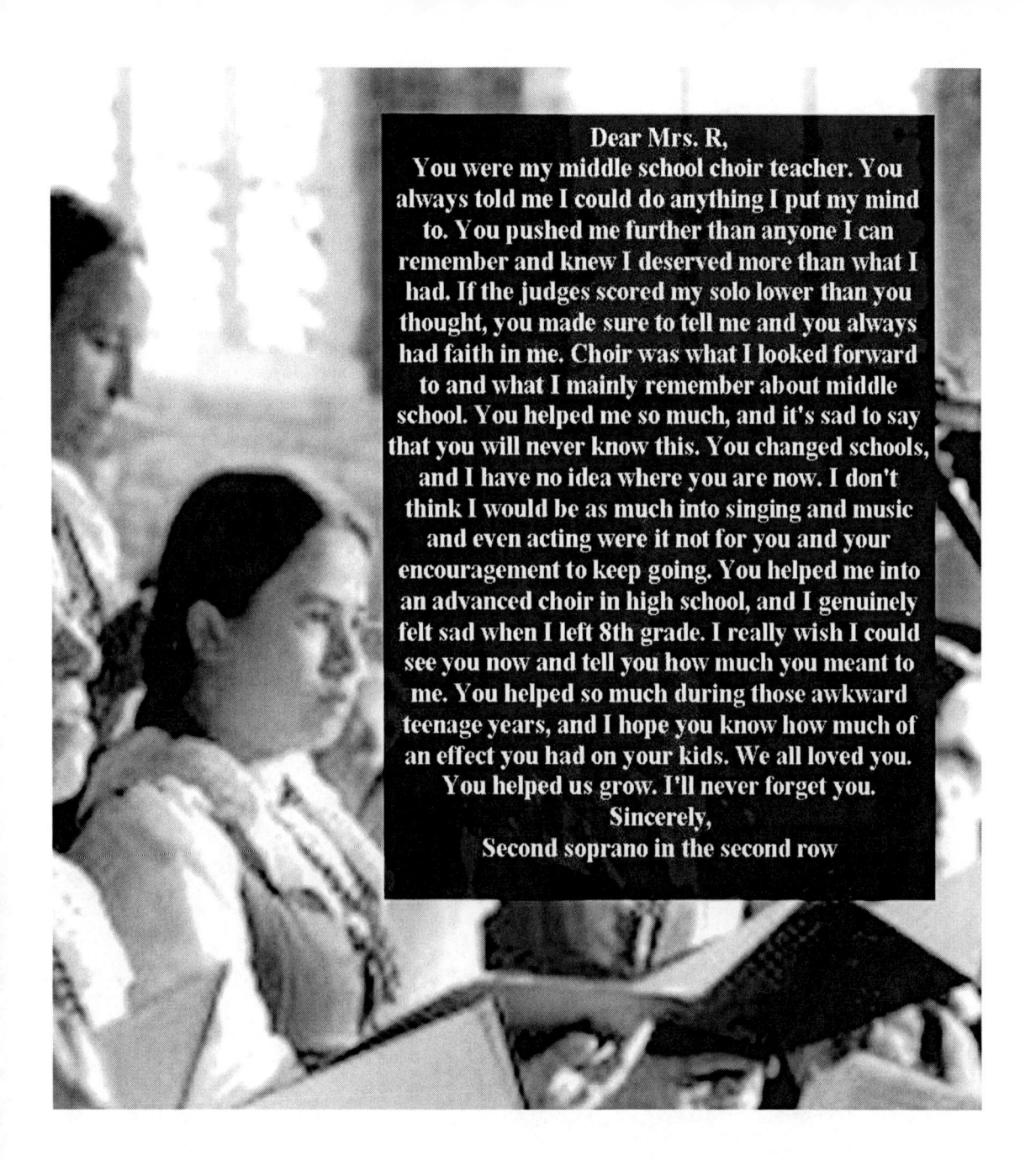

Dear Mr. I. Kant,
Napoleon was a bip bap boooop skidderydooooo. Quick, argue with that.
I thank you for your time and look forward to imagining your response.

Your little bug boy,

F. Kafka

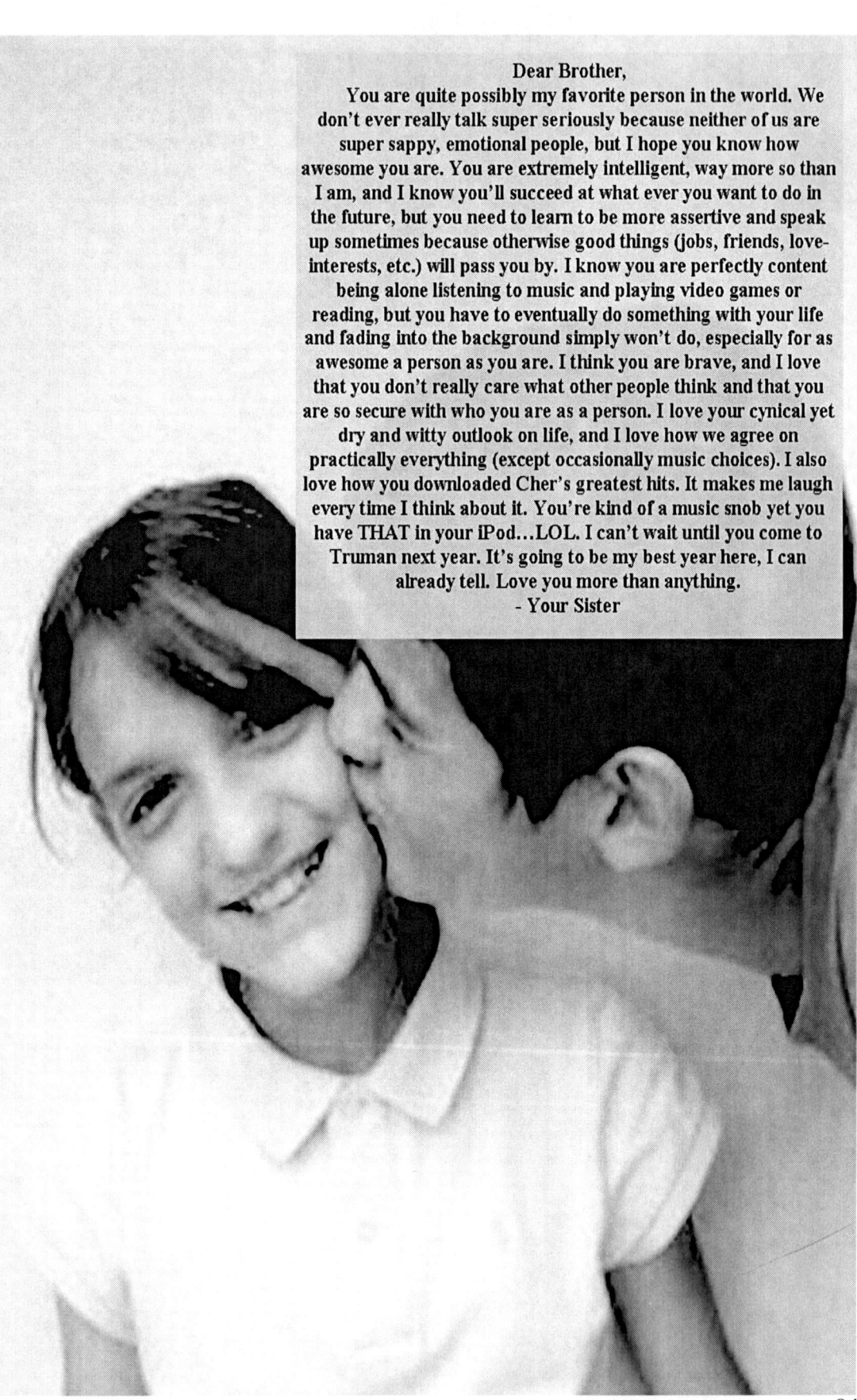

Dear Brother,
You are quite possibly my favorite person in the world. We don't ever really talk super seriously because neither of us are super sappy, emotional people, but I hope you know how awesome you are. You are extremely intelligent, way more so than I am, and I know you'll succeed at what ever you want to do in the future, but you need to learn to be more assertive and speak up sometimes because otherwise good things (jobs, friends, love-interests, etc.) will pass you by. I know you are perfectly content being alone listening to music and playing video games or reading, but you have to eventually do something with your life and fading into the background simply won't do, especially for as awesome a person as you are. I think you are brave, and I love that you don't really care what other people think and that you are so secure with who you are as a person. I love your cynical yet dry and witty outlook on life, and I love how we agree on practically everything (except occasionally music choices). I also love how you downloaded Cher's greatest hits. It makes me laugh every time I think about it. You're kind of a music snob yet you have THAT in your iPod…LOL. I can't wait until you come to Truman next year. It's going to be my best year here, I can already tell. Love you more than anything.
- Your Sister

Dear Ashish,

I never really got around to telling you this, but I love you no matter what. You were annoying at times, especially at the times when we used to hang out, you were a show-off and very controlling with me. I know you did it out of love, and you were trying to protect me and trying to act like my possessive older brother. We were family friends, but it is quite amazing how you embraced me as a little sister from the first time we officially met. After that you always acted like a brother. The students in my high school teased me for being related to you, you were not the most popular kid around but that did not matter to me for I knew that you cared for me and that was what mattered the most.

You toned down your bossiness and boastfulness in the later years, and we did not hang out much by then, mainly because you went to India to complete high school while I left for Thailand. But whenever we met I could see that you still cared. The first time we saw each other after ages there was glee in your face that I will never forget, and you introduced me to your girlfriends, which was a surprise for me because I never really thought you would settle down with someone. And I introduced you to my boyfriend who coincidently had the same full name as yours, and you did give him the suspicious look. But you guys managed to get together well.

Now you are gone, away from this world. It is sad to see because you were one of the few people I had grown up with and you loved life and lived your life like there was no tomorrow. And I am glad you did that, glad that you went on trips and took chances and even climbed a certain portion of Mount Everest before you left the world.

Some things I never got to tell you though. Before we officially met I knew you already and had a huge crush on you. But you were 16 and I was 14 then and obviously you completely ignored me. But when I grew up and we were introduced by our parents at a party you would not stop talking to me. By this point I had lost interest in you already, but it felt good not to be ignored. After that you came in the same high school that I was in. And we loved each other like cousins. The best part was I was a bigger part of your life than some of my friends who would always brag about being your friend when you were in your ignoring me phase.

We were ridiculed in school especially because you were trying to keep me away from most of my friends because you did not think they were good enough for me, the worse was when one of the girls accused me of flirting with you in the presence of my boyfriend. Remember, the time I came with my boyfriend and one other girl and boy? Well, we got into a huge fight, and she called me a slut and that he has seen me in action with you. I think she was jealous because I was close to you and physical affection of any kind is taken negatively in our society. Plus, how could I flirt with you, I have taken you in like a cousin already and my boyfriend was there beside me that night. What can I say, you were a charming guy, and ladies did like you.

After I came to the states, your dad sent you to Thailand so you could study and transfer to the states like me. Your father really wanted you to be more like me. Unfortunately fate has something else in store for you, and you left us. However, I feel like you are my guardian, and you keep me away from all the negativity. I love you like a cousin, and I will miss your presence in my life.

With lots of love,
Krisha

Hey Nugget,

I was thinking today about when we were in high school, when you were all messed up. Sometimes I think about all the things I should've told mom. The things I didn't realize were signs. Remember the time you broke the ruler on my leg? I should've told her then. I'm sorry, but I was so young and so weak. Remember when you used to talk to grandma and Michael after they died? I should've told mom then, I'm sorry that I didn't. I didn't know how much pain you were in! Remember when I saw you steal that bottle of Tylenol? I should've told mom then, but I had no idea how much trouble you were in. I love you so much. It hurts me to know that I didn't do anything. I'm so sorry I resented you for so many years. The time you tried to push mom down the stairs I hated you. I'm sorry, but mom was my only friend then. That day you told me to kill myself? I thought about it. I really did. That's how much I love you. I thought how I'd let you down and how much I wanted you to approve of me. Em called then, she stopped me. I'm sorry, but sometimes I think it would've been better if she hadn't called. I know you'd yell at me for saying that, but that's the truth. That's why I keep a picture of you and me from last Christmas by my bed. Remind me of all the good times. I'm sorry I can't keep secrets anymore; I don't want to see anyone go through what I saw you go through. I love you big sister. I love you so much that sometimes I'm afraid of disappointing you. I know, when you're in a good mood, I could never do you wrong, but you scare me when you're mad. I know you'll come out of it, but sometimes I see Dad and that scares me. I know when you see Dad in our brother that it scares you. I'm sorry but sometimes I get scared of what to say to you. I feel like I can't really say what I feel to you because you might get mad. I love you, and I only want the best for you. I am so sad that you got all of our families problems. I am so grateful you shielded me for so long, but I'm an adult now. Remember that time you were driving me home, and you told me that no matter what happened I was to never commit suicide? What you didn't know was that I had been, since I was 6. I remember holding a knife to my wrist when I was six and thinking how easy it would be to just end it. I have never told anyone that, not even you. I know I don't come visit you enough, but that's because I'm scared. The good times are the best days of my life, but the bad days just take me back to a place I never want to go again, home. I hate that you feel bad about the way you shaped me. You were one of the major creators in my personality. Our siblings all think they know the way to get you out of a bad day, but they don't. They don't know you like I do. We were so close, I'm sorry I drew away. I know it was my fault. You only want to be closer to me, and I'm too scared. I'm scared of getting hurt again. You think that when you have a bad day that I'm just extra quiet, but that's not it at all. Nugget, when you feel bad I feel TERRIBLE. It eats me up inside. My throat swells with holding back the tears. Remember that day last summer when I was visiting and our brother wanted to go to lunch, and it was stressing you out? Remember when I cried, and you yelled at me? You want to know why I cried? Because I love you, and I hate to see you in so much pain. If I could give my life to take away your disease, I would in a second. You don't realize how much it affects me, or even how much it affects you. I miss you. I love you. I hope you know that.
With All of My Love,
G-Unit

Dear Mom, Vanessa, and Jenny,

This is your fat daughter/sister, Anneliese. I just wanted to tell you that I resent you three. Want to know why? How about every single day with the constant reminder about how fat I am or how the only reason I like coming with you to the grocery store is to stuff my face and become fatter. I'm not mad at Dad, Zac, or Nick (brothers). They never make fun of me for who I am. They're smart and know not to talk about a girl and her weight because they're mature and understand.

I resent you though, Mom, Vanessa, and Jenny (sisters). You're the reason I've come to dislike most girls because all they seem to do is talk and gossip about people and become hateful.

Mom, I understand you were once skinny and beautiful when you were young, but now, your metabolism has slowed, and you have no right to tell me that I'm a cow and bear and will never find a man that would love me for being overweight.

Vanessa, how dare you make fun of me for eating when you eat 10x more than me and are lucky to have a fast metabolism although you've NEVER been involved in any sport/outdoor activity whereas I've been in track for two years and still get made fun of for not being skinny like you, my older sister. By the way, your comeback "fat, ugly pig" got old the first 1,000 times you said it, but it's not like it still doesn't hurt every time you say it.

Jenny, you are a hateful person. It seems as though every day you have to make fun of me for being fat if I don't let you borrow something or you get annoyed with me. You tell me that I'm a "fat bitch" and I need to "go lose weight" even though you, mom, and Vanessa know that I cry like a wimp every time you hurt me and then continue to make fun of me by asking if you had "hurt my feelings" or if I'm going to go run to my room and cry more.

I know that I'm annoying and not mean, but for you guys to make fun of me on an every-day basis is a low blow. I KNOW I'm fat. I KNOW I need to lose weight. Don't you think I've tried? I've tried eating healthier but now that Mom stopped cooking and tells Vanessa to go buy fast food every day it gets pretty hard. I do resist the temptations but you (Jenny) and Vanessa saying things like "oh are you trying to lose weight, how cute" is not very motivational.

Lucky for me, I'm strong enough to never consider suicide/bulimia/anorexia because I love my life and the people I've met who don't treat me the way you guys do. Fortunately for you, however, you know my weak point and take great pride in making fun of me whenever you can because you want to feel better about yourself. I bet it hurts to know that mom and dad consider me the favorite because I always talk to them, do well in school and want and appreciate them.

I just can't wait for the day when karma takes its toll and you two finally know how it feels to be called fat and made fun of and realize how much you hurt me and put me through for 17 years of my life. And by the looks of the past few years, it seems as though both of you are gaining some butt and stomach, so you won't be able to make much fun of me anymore. The only thanks you'll deserve one day is for making me a stronger person and allowing me to go on and teach my children how to treat everyone with respect, no matter how big or small.

I love all of you guys, I really do. But, Vanessa and Jenny, how do you expect to become psychologists some day when you don't even have the competence to understand what it's like to hurt someone the way you do? You know how much I've cried and suffered every day of my fat life, but yet you go and major in psychology and become involved in protests (Vanessa) helping other people feel better about themselves and once you get home, you're both hypocrites once again and make fun of me.

I really pray for you to stop making fun of me, and I take back what I said. I don't wish you being fat like me, ever. I just want you to know that you hurt me and even though I hope nothing happens to you guys, karma is a bitch, no matter what.

Dear Grandpa Burt,

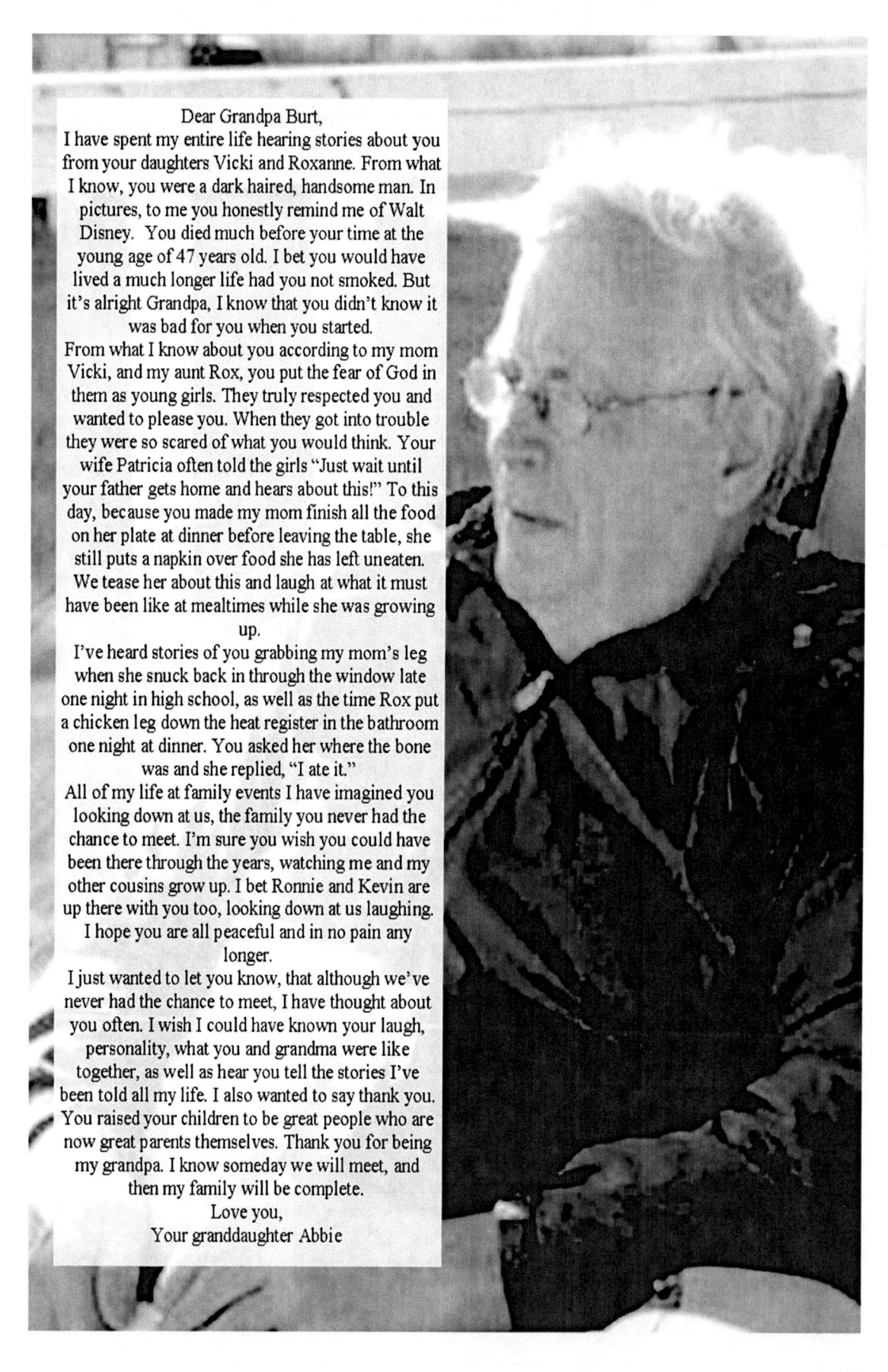

I have spent my entire life hearing stories about you from your daughters Vicki and Roxanne. From what I know, you were a dark haired, handsome man. In pictures, to me you honestly remind me of Walt Disney. You died much before your time at the young age of 47 years old. I bet you would have lived a much longer life had you not smoked. But it's alright Grandpa, I know that you didn't know it was bad for you when you started.

From what I know about you according to my mom Vicki, and my aunt Rox, you put the fear of God in them as young girls. They truly respected you and wanted to please you. When they got into trouble they were so scared of what you would think. Your wife Patricia often told the girls "Just wait until your father gets home and hears about this!" To this day, because you made my mom finish all the food on her plate at dinner before leaving the table, she still puts a napkin over food she has left uneaten. We tease her about this and laugh at what it must have been like at mealtimes while she was growing up.

I've heard stories of you grabbing my mom's leg when she snuck back in through the window late one night in high school, as well as the time Rox put a chicken leg down the heat register in the bathroom one night at dinner. You asked her where the bone was and she replied, "I ate it."

All of my life at family events I have imagined you looking down at us, the family you never had the chance to meet. I'm sure you wish you could have been there through the years, watching me and my other cousins grow up. I bet Ronnie and Kevin are up there with you too, looking down at us laughing.

I hope you are all peaceful and in no pain any longer.

I just wanted to let you know, that although we've never had the chance to meet, I have thought about you often. I wish I could have known your laugh, personality, what you and grandma were like together, as well as hear you tell the stories I've been told all my life. I also wanted to say thank you. You raised your children to be great people who are now great parents themselves. Thank you for being my grandpa. I know someday we will meet, and then my family will be complete.

Love you,
Your granddaughter Abbie

Dear Son:

You are almost 19 now, old enough to understand that people do not always act in a rational manner. We are not close now and your mother wants you to come live with me. I find this ironic when from the point of the divorce until just recently your mother did her best to limit my time with you. In every major decision in your life she has fought me. I had to take her to court to increase my visitation with you to 2 days a week instead of one. She took every opportunity she could to keep you away from me. Now she wants you to come live with me. Please trust me when I say I did everything in my power to fight her and spend time with you. It took me years to pay off the mountain of debt she accumulated during our marriage; unfortunately the financial situation she is in right now is due to her own financial irresponsibility. She can rip me off, lie to me and saddle me with debt but the IRS and the bank that holds her mortgage are a different story. They have lawyers and will
readily take her to court, unlike her ex-husband. I am sad for you but can not and will not help her. Sadly as they say it is time for her to pay the piper, her chickens have come home to roost, she has made her bed and now she must lie in it. Whatever the cliché, she is not a victim, she has only herself to blame.

I will always be there for you

Love
Your Dad

dear my family and my best friend,

dear my mom, thanks for everything, you're the one.
dear my dad, i know you've been trying so hard but you still can't be a great dad, your son need your attention but you are not always available for him.
dear my bro, be a drummer or play soccer.
dear my sister, i hate you cause you never help me, your life just you and your boy friend, I'm still here.
dear my grandma, i may never see your face, but every time i remember you i cry cause my parents won't bring me to your grave..
dear my grandpa, i never have your picture, i always wonder how your looks.
dear all of my entire family, i think I'm broken home though my parents didn't divorce.
and for my best friend..thanks for the shoulder, for the understand, for make me calm down while I'm on my temper, thanks for dancing with me when i play great DJ - the ting tings,thanks for support me. so sorry I'm being selfish and sometimes i'm annoying you all and thanks for hang out at mc donalds and being crazy there. while i write this, i imagine your smiles, your laugh, your sad. and when i want to suicide, yeah i know , that's really stupid thing but you saved me. i can't count how much you have been saved me. sorry being childish , i just can't hold anymore. i want to be with you all but i have to go somewhere which i can found new life with new people.

-your daughter,granddaughter,best friend

Little Brother,

We never told you what was going on. For years you watched as I tore the family into pieces, leaving you alone and confused. Mom and Dad, they just didn't think you'd understand. I didn't want to talk about it. Little Brother, I love you so much. I really regret not being able to be there for you until later. I know that dealing with me wasn't easy. The mood swings and crazy times. My only regret in life is that I spent so many years ignoring you. You didn't deserve it. You shouldn't have had to live through that like you did.

Do you remember two years ago, September? When I first told you about whom I really was? I remember. I remember watching you cry in that soft way that all of us do. When you told me that you knew I was dying, but thought I was dying from cancer, it broke my heart. Suicide attempts, depression, those are things I wish you never had to be exposed to. Watching you cry was the worst thing I've ever seen, and being the cause of those tears was the worst thing I've ever done.

Little Brother, I'm so sorry. I know things haven't been easy for you. I know I caused a lot of hurt for you, and the rest of our family. But I hope you know that I love you. I hope you know you are one of the only reasons I'm able to push through the tough days.

I also hope that we never have to go through any suicidal thoughts or actions anymore. It's hard for me to forgive myself for what I put you through. Mom and Dad understood, but it is hard to tell a 7th grader that you want nothing more than to lie down and end it. I'm so sorry I made you cry. I'm so sorry I caused you worry and hurt. Little Brother, I love you so much, and I never want you to suffer like that by my doing again.

I've written a poem for you. One day I'll let you read it.

Keep up the guitar, you'll go places. Who knows, maybe you'll be the next Tod A.

I love you Little Brother.

-Your Sister.

Dear Family,

I can't be your crutch. I cannot be the one you lean on when things go wrong. I'm too young. I don't have all the answers. I don't know if that's what you really expect from me, but I don't ask questions for a reason. I want to know what's important. That's it. I can't be the glue.
Stop living through me, just live.

Me

Dear You,

    I guess I will make this short and sweet because there really is not much to say. I am not completely sure why you are still with him. Immediately after the incident, the only road I imagined you taking was to get a divorce, as you probably should have. I said I didn't care when I was sixteen because you asked the both of us in person what you should do, and that is not our decision, though it probably should have been an easy one. By the way, my mom wasn't happy you talked to us without her knowing. Now that I am getting older, and it is five years later I honestly thought I wouldn't care but I guess I care more. I think it is bullshit that the both of you still come around Grandma and that she stands behind you instead of my mom and sister. He isn't ever going to be a part of the family anymore, so I hope you aren't waiting for that time to roll around. Unfortunately, I thought I could deal with you and him separately, but because you are just so dedicated to him, it makes me not want to be around you too. That's why we didn't come out to your place last month, and that's why I didn't really care if we got to have lunch together. I think your decision was wrong, and you should have had a little more respect for yourself than to stay with him. So what if it was going to be hard to get a divorce, at least you would have done the right thing. Anyway, I know this is going to get nowhere as you have made your decision. I just know that if I were ever in your position I would have known immediately what to do, and it would have been an easy decision. I am sure next time I see you I'll act like everything is fine, but I know this issue is going to come up some time or another, and I won't be nice about it.

-Me

Dear Alex,
I know you already know this, but I want the world to know what I do about my Baby Sister! I think you are the most amazingly talented, kind-hearted person I have ever had the pleasure to know! I'm so proud of you for all your accomplishments you've made, and I know even more great things are to come for you! You are amazing, and I'm just glad you didn't follow in my footsteps. I know I wasn't the best roll-model, but I hope you learned a lot about what NOT to do from watching me screw up my whole life! I'm SO proud of you!! You inspire me to want to do better for me and my Baby that will be here soon! I Love you, and thanks for being You!!!

LoVe YoUr BiG SiS

Dear Brazil,

I've always been kind of in love with you. From the first night I saw you, I knew. You didn't say a word because you were shy back then, but I immediately thought "Oh no, this one could be trouble for me." During my relationship with my boyfriend all year, I suppressed how attracted I was to you, and I tormented myself over it. The things that come out of your mouth inspire me to search for myself, to be myself, and rejoice in who I am. Exactly as I am, unedited. I wanted to be one of the reasons you stayed in America. I also wanted to help you not be depressed anymore. I wanted to know that I was priceless and irreplaceable, and you proved it to me. You weren't afraid to TELL me that I was, and there was never hesitation in your voice. You were sure that I was crucial to the universe, and you told me why and how the world needs me. Thank you for giving me the encouragement, support, and hugs that I needed in order to make my tough decision yesterday. I believe God put you in my life (whether you believe in Him or not) to help me discover myself, and I'm so thankful.

Sincerely,
Bird in the Night

Dear John Kelley

Recently, life has been somewhat horrendous to you. You lost a job and, shortly thereafter, lost your children and then your wife. My previous letter may have been somewhat early. Having thought extensively about the subject, I have decided that Liz is extremely selfish, with no real regard for what would be best for the whole but only what would be best for her. To take kids out of their school in the middle of the year has to be so psychologically traumatizing that I can't even begin to fathom the damage she might have caused. Now, she acts like her life sucks in St. Louis because she has to live with Sheryl but she chose that life. Any sane person could have told her that things would get ridiculously tense, especially with a passive-aggressive brother-in-law. I am writing to say that you still have people on your side. Your children leap to your defense the second a conversation starts that is about you. I just want you to know that no one has forgotten you and that you will always be our father.

Sincerely,

Your son

Dear Mark,
I'm sorry for breaking you.
I remember your sob over the phone,
A shudder I could scarcely hear, not quite masked by the static.
And then I thought it was crazy,
But now it makes me ache
Because I finally know what it's like to be in love.
I've never lost it,
Never been told so nonchalantly that my everything is nothing anymore.
I can imagine though.

Maybe I've just gone sappy, but I read that letter again,
The one that came in the mail the day after I did it.
It made even me
(Once heartless heartbreaker)
A little tight in the throat, shaky in the hands.
The silly rhymes and the way you signed it in sloppy script
"With all my love"
Finally got to me I guess.
See, I thought it was over at the end of summer when I said,
"I hope I see you again someday,"
Knowing I probably wouldn't.
How could I have known that in your tucked-away musings, I was
it?

But you should know I think about you
Every other day or even more.
And you should know I wish for you
Constantly.
I wish for you a girl who melts over those azure eyes,
Like shattered glass,
Like I did.
I hope she enjoys fireworks and fireflies,
Long walks and the Red Hot Chili Peppers,
And doesn't mind you're quiet.
Maybe she'll make you braver
And you'll squeeze her fingers,
Kiss her temple,
And tell her you love her before you lose her,
And she'll put you back together.

With all my best wishes, as lame as that sounds,
Kelly

Dear Fake Best Friend,

I hope my decision to write this letter and the reason why you are mad at me are worth it because I can no longer stomach the run around that you are giving me. I have no doubt that what I did or said is completely worthy of this treatment but I cannot sit here and let you dangle you giving me the silent treatment or being angry at me as a way to make me feel inferior to you. We are suppose to be on equal footing here and you are always telling me that if there's a problem between two people then the two people just need to be honest and upfront with each other which is not something that you do with me, you make me feel inferior by ignoring me. You pride yourself on the fact that you're so honest with people and that you can call your friends out on their bullshit while still remaining friends with them, you're not honest M, you're fake.

I'm sick of wondering if you're not talking to me because you're busy or because you're angry at me, because it's been happening more frequently since spring break. You ignore me when were out and other people take notice and it's not fair when I have to explain to people or make excuses for why you are being so rude to me. I'm sick of making excuses for how you treat me, it's not fair.

This sucks that there is three weeks of school left and I feel like we may graduate not being friends, which would be a shame but I feel very uneasy about this situation. I can't apologize for something that I am unaware of what I did but I would be willing to talk to you about it. I can't promise that it will change anything but an explanation of why you're treating me like this would be nice.

Honestly I can't be friends with someone who uses situations like this to punish my by not talking to me for days at a time. It's not fair to either one of us and I deserve to be friends with someone who treats me better than this. You use to tell me how my roommates were such fake friends and caused so many problems between us but they never made me feel like this. We are not acting like friends and I know we have a lot going on with graduating, looking for jobs and applying to law school but friends make time for each other no matter what, you make time for R and M, why not me? I don't want to be fighting with someone every other week or worrying when you'll get mad at me next and about what, since you never tell me why you're mad you just give me the silent treatment.

So, I guess if you ever do try to talk to me again I will probably tell you that I've thought long and hard about what to say and I don't care why you're mad at me because ignoring me and treating me like shit isn't something that a true friend would do. A true friend would tell me what happened and try to talk about it with me. You are not a true friend and our friendship is over!

Sincerely,

Your Ex Best Friend

Dear girl who sits in the front row,

I saw the way you looked at him and how eagerly you offered to let him borrow your pen, but I got there first in both the literal and figurative sense.
I saw the way you batted your eyes and heard you laugh too loud at his jokes and try to say something brilliant to impress him. Unfortunately for you, he wasn't even listening--he and I were too busy having our own private conversation.
You seem like a nice girl, but you should probably stop trying because in the end, I was the one walking home with him, and all you got was an unfortunate nickname.

Love,
The girl who sits in the second row

Dear ex-friend,

There are so many things I would like to tell you, though not all of them are pleasant.

I'd like to start off by saying how angry I am with you. We were best friends, once. We talked about everything and shared our most inner hopes and fears, but you still felt the need to lie to me. You lied about a lot of things. Looking back, I can't even define what was truth and what was a lie. This is why I cut off contact with you. If you really were a true friend to me, you wouldn't feel the need to lie about everything. You made me feel like an idiot. Did you actually think that I swallowed your lies? Some of them were so ridiculous, so unbelievable that I had to wonder if you thought that I - and our other friends - were stupid.

Second, there was the drama you felt the need to cause. It was like you lived on it; there always had to be something that put you in the spot light. You could never be happy. Being around you was draining and sometimes depressing.

The only way I could escape the drama and the lies was to never speak to you again, to never see you. My life has been happier, filled with love and laughs rather than lies and tears, though I must admit, sometimes I look back at the good times we had, and I miss you. When you weren't lying to me, you were so fun and loving, but I wonder if that was all a lie too.

I'm not completely blaming you for the demise of our friendship, because I know I'm at fault too. I simply didn't put an effort into our relationship, partly because I was tired of hearing what you would come up with next, but mostly because of the boyfriend I ditched you for. I have to say though, that the one I've been with for 2 years now is worth the end of our friendship. I chose him over you and don't regret it in the slightest.

I hope someday that you'll come to realize that you don't need to come up with lies to be happy, and maybe when that day comes we can be friends again.

Dear You,

I love you. You're one of my best friends, and I care so much about you.

But I'm scared for you.

You don't take your medications anymore.

Every time you call, I fear that it's not going to be you on the other line. I'm afraid that it's going to be a paramedic desperately seeking a friend or family member to tell them that their loved one has killed himself.

Everything you've told me has stayed between us. I would never betray your trust, but I worry about you. I can tell you're no longer happy.

You've fallen out of love with your girlfriend. You've told me this personally. You might have been drunk at the time, but I know it's the truth. You don't look at her the same way you used to. I don't care how long you've been dating and if your family and friends expect you to get married. She's not the one for you.

Those nights we stayed up late, just you and me, talking, listening to "Konstantine" play on repeat…those nights mean more to me than I can ever say.

When I woke up that one morning, my head on your shoulder and your head on mine, our fingers intertwined - I'd never felt such love and intimacy in a friendship before.

We've shared so much together, and I can't imagine my life without you, so this is my one request to you:

LOVE YOURSELF AGAIN!

Take care of yourself. I want to see you happy, and not just because you're drunk. You're better than that.

Go back to university and finish your degree. Follow through with your dreams. You, of all people, deserve to see them come true.

I love you, and I hope you can do the same someday.

Love,
Me

Dear Grandpa,

I am twenty-two years old, and even though you're still alive I've only met you twice. Once when I was five, it was my birthday and you smelled bad, and the other time I was ten when the whole family came to visit you and grandma in Florida, but I was too preoccupied with the opportunity to go to Disney World that I took little notice of you. I know you through the generic birthday cards you religiously send every year accompanied with a check for twenty dollars and through the ongoing stories of my mother's childhood that she is just now letting me get a glimpse into. The stories always frame you has a bastard of a man; one who is frugal and strict. You apparently have the same station wagon that who had in the 1970s, and your home doesn't have air conditioning. Yet here I sit typing away on a keyboard that is placed on your old desk. The wood is faded and worn now, but it is still beautiful and forever classic. When I moved it into my apartment a couple of years ago I found an old picture of you and grandma in black and white. You are in a military uniform; I think it's from the air force. Mom said you had been in the Korean War as a navigator, I'm sad will never get to fully understand your experiences in an environment of war. I still have the picture. It remains in the same compartment I found it, as sort of homage to my grandfather.

 My dad doesn't like you very much. He says you left my mother all alone in St. Louis when she was 18, while you set off to the Sunshine State. Her early twenties as I understand them were a pretty rough time, full of constant layoffs from work. But I think you're a good a man. You helped us out financially when dad got sick and had to quit his job. We didn't go hungry because of you, and I will forever be grateful.

Thank you,
Your Grandson

Dear Janitor,

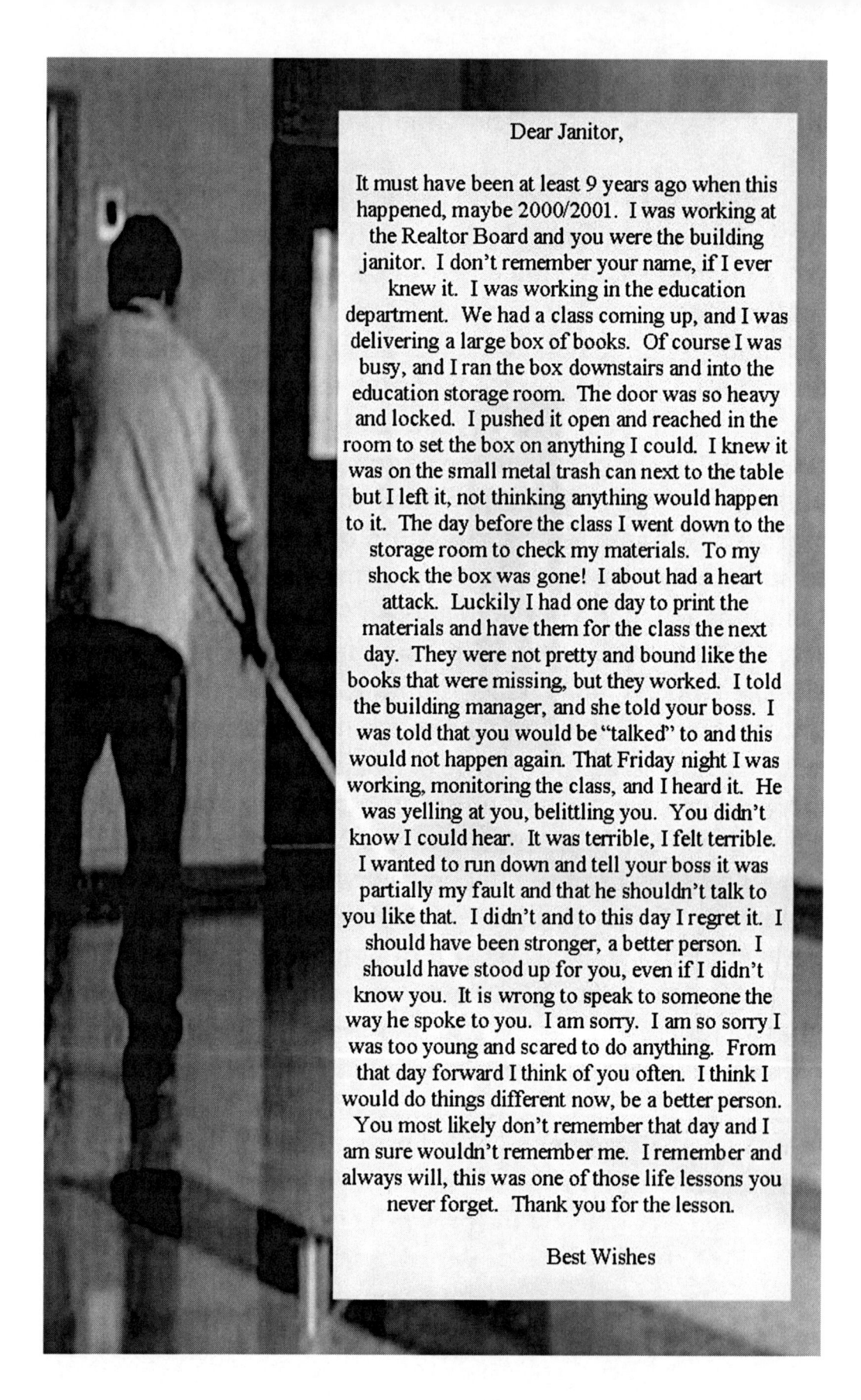

It must have been at least 9 years ago when this happened, maybe 2000/2001. I was working at the Realtor Board and you were the building janitor. I don't remember your name, if I ever knew it. I was working in the education department. We had a class coming up, and I was delivering a large box of books. Of course I was busy, and I ran the box downstairs and into the education storage room. The door was so heavy and locked. I pushed it open and reached in the room to set the box on anything I could. I knew it was on the small metal trash can next to the table but I left it, not thinking anything would happen to it. The day before the class I went down to the storage room to check my materials. To my shock the box was gone! I about had a heart attack. Luckily I had one day to print the materials and have them for the class the next day. They were not pretty and bound like the books that were missing, but they worked. I told the building manager, and she told your boss. I was told that you would be "talked" to and this would not happen again. That Friday night I was working, monitoring the class, and I heard it. He was yelling at you, belittling you. You didn't know I could hear. It was terrible, I felt terrible. I wanted to run down and tell your boss it was partially my fault and that he shouldn't talk to you like that. I didn't and to this day I regret it. I should have been stronger, a better person. I should have stood up for you, even if I didn't know you. It is wrong to speak to someone the way he spoke to you. I am sorry. I am so sorry I was too young and scared to do anything. From that day forward I think of you often. I think I would do things different now, be a better person. You most likely don't remember that day and I am sure wouldn't remember me. I remember and always will, this was one of those life lessons you never forget. Thank you for the lesson.

Best Wishes

Dear N,

For some reason, I have been thinking about you a lot lately. I can't quite put my finger on it. Maybe it is because if things went according to plan, we would be married right about now. Maybe it is because you are gone. I'm not sure. Some thoughts are quite pleasant and some are not. When I think about you, I always wonder what would happen if I would have spoken up early on about my feelings instead of trying to hide or compromise them. Or what would happen if I would have kept the game going and settled for you.

I wonder what would happen if we were to speak, to have a real conversation about our lives now. Would you forgive me? Would I forgive you? I'm not sure. I wonder what it would be like to have you back in my life, and I cannot decide if I would want that or not. So when I sat down to write this letter, I thought for sure all the answers would spill out. I don't have any answers. I thought for sure I would want to be your friend, but I'm not sure I do. After over a year, you have yet to contact me, so I guess I have your response. So this is it, I guess. Best of luck to you in all you do. I'm sure you will be fine. I'm sure I will, too.

Here if you want to reach out,

J

Dear You,

When you said "No one can make me do something I don't want" I just about tripped over the irony of the words actually hitting home when you said them instead of when so many other people have said them.

Of course I was going to fall for you after that.

Of course.

Sincerely,
Me.

Dear You,

Boy and girl meet. Boy and girl fall in love. Boy goes on holiday. Boy meets new girl. Boy and new girl fall in love. Boy breaks old girl's heart. Boy and new girl get married.

The end . . .

No it's not the end. I was the old girl. And every day I feel the pain of being treated like I was the one who did something wrong. I spent 3 months waiting for you. You on the other hand went and cheated.

In all this time did you ever think about me?! I still think about you.

Not because I want to be with you, God knows I am better off without you, but because of the things you made me realize. When I was with you I hated myself. I felt fat and ugly and stupid and useless. I was ashamed of who I was because I thought I was the lucky one to have you in my life.

I was so devoted to you. I thought we would be together forever.

I realized this summer that none of that is true and that I am glad it isn't so. I am beautiful inside and out. I have wonderful curves which I am proud to have. I am clever enough to now realize that you are scum and I am not. And I CAN do anything I put my mind too.

I am a person who deserves the very best. You were not good enough for me. You didn't realize what you had.

One of these days I will find a man who will walk hundreds of miles bare foot in a rainstorm just because they miss my face. Because I AM a better person without you.

The old Girl

Dear HF,

Everyday, I try to go by your classroom just to take a peek at you. I know it sounds a little freaky, but I get this weird, overwhelming happiness whenever you say hi to me. I love your beautiful green eyes, your warm smile, your super-hot bod, your sweet voice. You see? you make me sound like Stephenie Meyer. But it's okay, I forgive you for inducing these feelings in me. What I don't know is if I'll ever be able to forget you. Because I don't know if you like me back. I really hope you do, my life would all just fall into place if you did. But it would seem so surreal. You're 3 years older than me. It's practically nothing, but in high school it's a big deal. And I'm just so shy when I'm around you, I can't be myself. And there are so many beautiful girls in your grade, why would you want me? I just get so insecure. But every night, I think about how great it would be to be in your arms, how amazing it would feel to kiss you. The great times we could have. I'm begging you, please, if you like me back, say so. If not, just ignore me so that it's easier for me to forget you. My heart can't take so much teasing. I long for you. This will be my little secret.

love always,

Dahlia ♥

Dear Daddy,

It should have been you.

The role of a stepfather has to be hard. You didn't get to experience the emotional rollercoaster of my birth, the joy of watching me take my first step or the intense surprise when the word "dad" came out of my mouth for the first time. You didn't get to hold the back of my bike when the training wheels came off and you didn't get to wipe away my tears when I scraped my knee.

The problem is that no stable father figure WAS there during those times. My sad excuse of a biological father was something to be less-than proud of and did not care whether I spoke his name or stubbed my toe.

Then you came into our lives. I can remember the first time I saw you. They say that little kids only remember events in their young lives that provoked intense emotions like fear and extreme excitement. I know that the reason why I remember that day is because somehow the 4-year-old in me knew you were someone who would change my life. The next memory I have of you is your marriage to my mom. It's weird how all the in between days don't even exist in my head.

Basically, I want to thank you for stepping in at exactly the right moment in my life. I'm sad that you weren't able to see the most important stepping-stones of my childhood, but really, you have been there for the most important part of every single day since you first walked into our lives, and I could not be happier.

This is my second attempt at writing you this letter and I still feel like it has not all been said. I don't know if I could express in words exactly how much I want to thank you and appreciate you. Even if you never read this, I hope you know that your DAUGHTER loves you.

Love you Dad,

Your Favorite

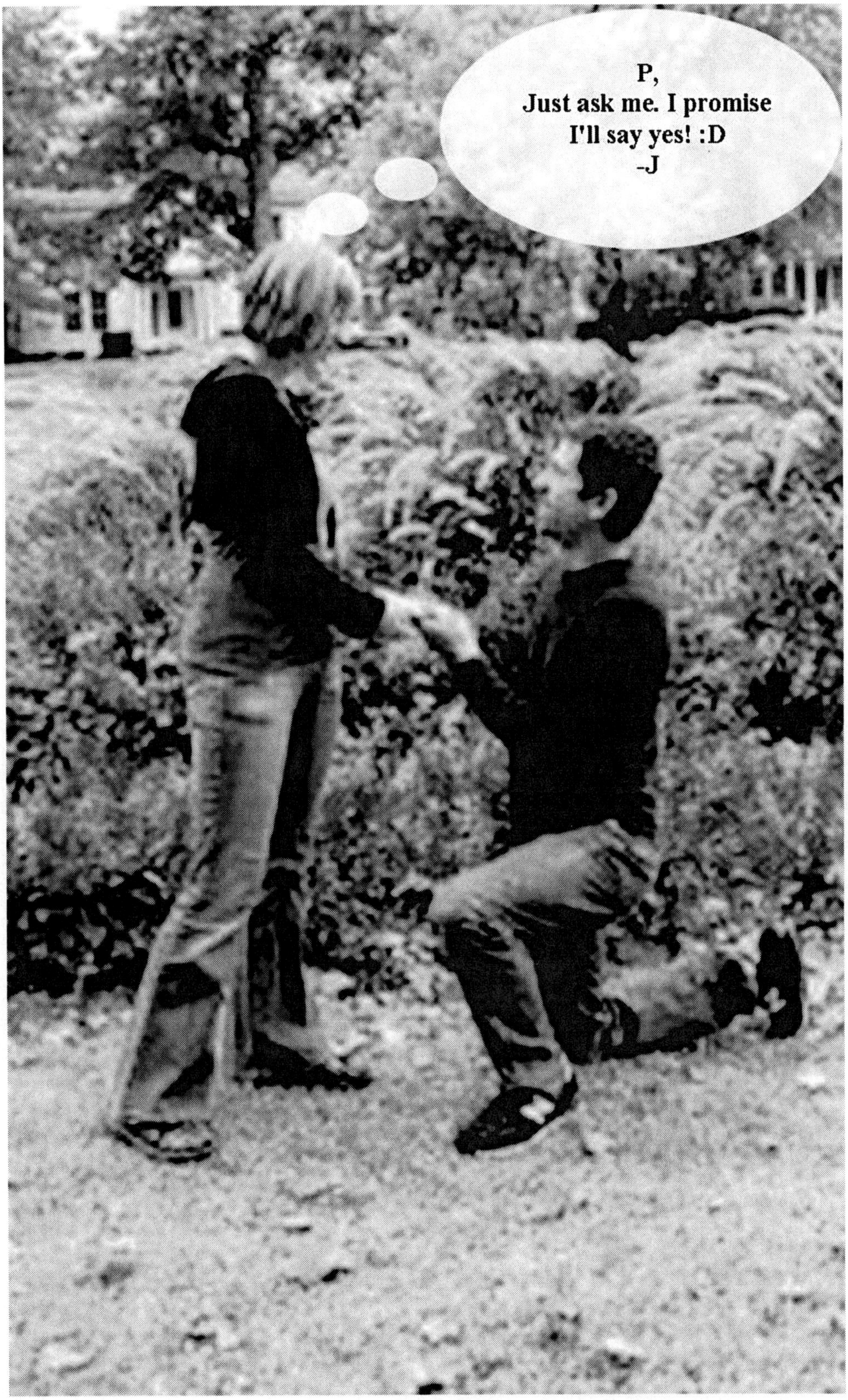
P,
Just ask me. I promise
I'll say yes! :D
-J

Check out Unwritten Letters Project's next endeavor

http://letters2ourfallenheroes.com

Alex Boles received inspiration for this project while attending Truman State University in northern Missouri. The project started with a few notes scribbled on a piece of notebook paper and ended up letting people around the world share their stories. She fully plans on continuing to update the website daily as well as start supplementary projects.

The next project from Unwritten Letters will be titled, "Letter to Our Fallen Heroes" and will include letters from the family members and friends of those who have fallen in their line of duty. This new project can be accessed from the original website unwrittenlettersproject.com.

Alex's next plans are to graduate from Truman State University in 2010 and apply to graduate programs for Creative Writing. She thanks everyone for their continued support in her project and future aspirations.

Her advice to you is to keep writing, keep expressing yourself creatively and don't let anyone try to silence your voice!